SpringerBriefs in Economics

For further volumes:
http://www.springer.com/series/8876

Gary Chaison

The New Collective Bargaining

Springer

Gary Chaison
Clark University
Worcester, MA, USA

ISSN 2191-5504 ISSN 2191-5512 (electronic)
ISBN 978-1-4614-4023-9 ISBN 978-1-4614-4024-6 (eBook)
DOI 10.1007/978-1-4614-4024-6
Springer New York Heidelberg Dordrecht London

Library of Congress Control Number: 2012939377

Printed on acid-free paper

Springer is part of Springer Science+Business Media (www.springer.com)

Acknowledgments

The author thanks Inderpreet (Preet) Shoker for her outstanding research assistance, and Clark University for providing financial assistance to the author as the 2009–2010 University Senior Faculty Fellow.

Contents

Chapter 1
Introduction: The New Collective Bargaining

Abstract The 2009 collective negotiations between the Boston Globe's management and the Newspaper Guild illustrate a new form of concession bargaining—*ultra-concession bargaining*. A key premise of this study is introduced; collective bargaining has been transformed in significant and new ways, and the implicit code of conduct between employers and unions has been eroded. The new collective bargaining is defined, and a distinction is drawn between conventional collective bargaining and concession bargaining. The two waves of concession bargaining (the first in the 1980s and the second in the years since the turn of this century) are briefly described.

Keywords Boston globe • New York Times company • Collective bargaining • Concession bargaining • Ultra-concession bargaining • Nonunion competition

In May 2009, collective bargaining between the Boston Globe and its unions broke down. And then we got a glimpse of a new, mean-spirited bargaining—ultra-concession bargaining.

The Boston Globe's parent company, the New York Times Company, responded to the bargaining impasse by taking an extreme hard line and threatening to either sell or close the Globe, New England's largest newspaper.[1] It demanded that the unions accept deep wage and benefit cuts. The company was in a shaky financial position and also asked workers at its flagship newspaper, the New York Times, to take a 5 % pay cut.

[1]For details on the 2009 negotiations between the Boston Globe and the New York Times Company—the employers—and the Newspaper Guild—the Globe's major union—see, for example: Boston Globe could file shut down notice Monday (2009), Gavin (2009), Gavin and O'Brien (2009), Kurtz (2009), Marks (2009), Perez-Pena (2009a, b, c), and What next for the Boston Globe? (2009).

G. Chaison, *The New Collective Bargaining*, SpringerBriefs in Economics,
DOI 10.1007/978-1-4614-4024-6_1,

In 1993, the Times Company had acquired the Globe for $1.1 billion. There were a few profitable years, but the Globe eventually suffered the shrinking circulation and financial losses so common to big-city newspapers that try to compete against suburban papers and the electronic media. The Globe lost nearly $50 million in 2008 and was on its way to losing $85 million the next year.

The Globe and its parent company tried to cut costs by using employee buyouts and layoffs to eliminate 50 full-time newsroom positions. But this was not enough and when the impasse in bargaining was reached, it looked like the 120-year old newspaper was near its end. The Times Company filed the legally required notices for mass layoffs and plant closings. It demanded wage cuts of $20 million annually from its four major operating unions; half would have to come from the Boston Newspaper Guild, the newspaper's largest union which represented editorial, advertising, and business office workers.

Management also insisted that the Guild relinquish lifetime job guarantees.[2] In collective bargaining 15 years earlier, the Guild received lifetime guarantees for 700 workers. By 2009 there were only 190 workers remaining with guarantees; the rest had either left or retired.

A tentative settlement cutting wages by 10 % was eventually reached but rejected in a close vote among the Guild's members (277 against vs. 265 for). The Guild's leadership had *not* endorsed the terms of the tentative settlement, something quite rare in collective bargaining. Union negotiators usually ask the membership to approve of tentative settlements that they reach at the bargaining table, staking their reputations as leaders and negotiators on ratification. But the Guild's officers thought they could do better in bargaining, and a majority of the union's members apparently agreed.

The Globe and the Times Company reacted to the contract rejection by imposing a 23 % wage cut. The union claimed that the company was being extremely hostile and punitive, and not bargaining in good faith; the company denied this and turned up the pressure by retaining an investment bank to find buyers for the Globe (O'Brien 2009).

As management cut wages on its own and threatened to sell the Globe, it looked like labor relations at the Globe had hit rock bottom and there could be no progress in further contract talks. But 2 weeks later, the union and management reached a tentative contract settlement that was endorsed by the Guild's officers and ratified by its members (by a vote of 366 for and 179 against). The 23 % wage cut imposed by the company was rolled back. Under the settlement there would be a 6 % wage cut, a freeze in the pension plan, reduced health care benefits, and a 5-day unpaid furlough; in all enough to give the Globe management what it wanted—a savings of $10 million per year. The lifetime job guarantees were eliminated.

[2]Lifetime employment at the Boston Globe protected against layoffs but not discharge for cause.

Why, after all the threats and anger, was an agreement finally reached and ratified? Apparently, the threat of shutting or selling the Globe made it clear that unless wages were rolled back and employment protections relaxed, jobs would be lost. For the workers, the settlement was far from the best settlement but at least jobs would be saved and their union would be around to bargain another day.

In October 2009, the Times Company announced that it would not sell the Globe after all—an attractive buyer could not be found and, with the wage and benefit cuts and end to job guarantees, the Globe no longer seemed like such an unbearable financial burden. Four months later, the Times Company reported that it had turned a corner—in its fourth quarter earnings had tripled, largely because of cost-cutting. The company's workforce had been reduced by about 20 %. In May 2011, it was announced that a Boston-area businessman was prepared to make an offer on the Globe (Ross 2011), but a sale never happened.

Do the troubled negotiations at the Globe show us the face of a new collective bargaining? Of course, a few might argue that no single case could truly reveal a new collective bargaining, that each negotiation has a unique character shaped by its history (past negotiations and agreements), context (the competitive position of the employer), and central characters (the personal bargaining styles of the negotiators). Bargaining at the Globe was undoubtedly shaped by the parent company's threats to sell or close the newspaper, the willingness of management to impose a severe wage cut after reaching an impasse, and the union leaders' refusal to endorse the tentative agreement. These are certainly unique features. But the Globe shows us what negotiations had become—an ultra-concession bargaining in which management forcefully acts and the union defensively reacts. Unions were now considered effective if they could make an orderly retreat and protect past gains. Employers were preoccupied controlling what the bargaining issues would be. Rather than being reluctant participants in collective bargaining, employers welcomed bargaining as a way to cut costs and relax work rules. Undoubtedly, what happened at the Globe was tough "hardball" bargaining—but that was what bargaining had become.

My basic premise is that collective bargaining has been transformed in significant and lasting ways and that the implicit code of conduct between employers and unions has been eroded. This decline of bargaining is symptomatic of the loss of union influence in the workplace and in the economy. We will explore the form and frequency of ultra-concession bargaining to develop a portrait of the new labor relations in America. But first we must distinguish between concession bargaining (or concessionary bargaining, as the term is sometimes used[3]) and conventional collective bargaining. We do that now.

Concessions are always made in the give and take of collective bargaining (Mitchell 1985). Unions and employers start with offers and demands that are

[3]Concession bargaining has also been called *concessionary bargaining*, *give-back bargaining*, *crisis bargaining*, and *reverse collective bargaining* (Chaison 2006; Cappelli 1983; Miner 1982; Rubenfeld 1983).

apart—sometimes far apart—and then the two move toward a middle ground by progressively offering more or demanding less. We call negotiators "shrewd" when they give up the least to get the most. Because concessions are expected by opponents in bargaining, negotiators ask for more than they really want or offer less than they plan to give so they can have some room to concede on terms. If stubborn and irrational negotiators refuse to ever make concessions, settlements would never be reached—there will just be the repetitious statement and restatement of positions without modification.

Although negotiators make concessions in conventional collective bargaining, in concession bargaining what they concede is nearly all one-sided and extraordinary in degree; unions are pressured to agree to terms that differ greatly from past settlements. They are asked to deviate from the patterns of past bargaining.[4] For instance, a union that normally gets a 2 or 3 % wage increase each year is told by the employer to settle for a wage freeze or even a wage cut; or a union must accept a lump-sum payment when it ratifies the agreement, instead of the more usual annual wage increase; or a union is pressured into a two-tiered wage system under which new hires will have lower wages or benefits than those doing the same work and presently employed.

Sometimes concession bargaining is only an isolated, temporary adjustment to economic hard times—a union's pragmatic response to an employer's demands that seem urgent and justifiable. But concession bargaining can also be a long-lasting and significant change in how unions and employers deal with each other. The first wave of concession bargaining during the late 1970s and the 1980s was mostly an employer and union adjustment to hard times—a way to reduce costs so jobs would not lost due to low-cost competition. This laid the foundation, however, for the second wave—the ultra-concession bargaining of the past decade with its lasting effect on the fundamentals of how unions and employers deal with each other.

The First Wave

The first wave of concession bargaining began in the late 1970s and intensified greatly in the early 1980s. Employers reacted to the pressures of low-cost competition from companies abroad (e.g., foreign steel and auto producers) and new entrants to previously regulated industries (e.g., the low-cost carriers in the once highly

[4] For example, concession bargaining has been defined in a legal webpage as "a kind of bargaining in which trade unions surrender or give back previously gained improvements in pay and conditions in exchange for some form of job security" (uslegal.com 2011). A dictionary of human resource management terms defined concession bargaining as "collective agreements in which trade unions surrender improvements in pay and conditions that they have previously secured in order to promote firm competiveness and protect employment" (Answers.com 2011).

regulated airline industry). Employers demanded cost-cutting settlements from unions. Many employers seemed desperate, fearing that their company's competitive health was at stake and that survival was assured only if their union gave them a break by agreeing to concessions in negotiations (Chaison 2006). A few employers, a small minority, simply found it lucrative to press for concessions even if these were not warranted by the company's financial health.

As we will see in the next chapter, concession bargaining was reported sporadically in the 1960s and 1970s (Henle 1973), but an identifiable wave became apparent by the start of the 1980s.[5] In the early and mid-1980s, there were wage freezes or cuts in 15–20 % of collective bargaining settlements, lump-sum payments in about a third, and two-tiered wage or benefit systems in more than 10 %. The first-year wage increases in bargaining settlements in 1982 averaged 2 % compared to 9 % in 1981. In a survey done by Business Week in May 1983, 26 % of unionized companies had received wage and benefit concessions from their unions (Concessionary bargaining: Will the new cooperation last? 1982). Throughout the 1980s, wage and benefit concessions spread to nearly half of the workers covered by collective bargaining agreements (Lewin et al. 2011).

Concession bargaining continued through the latter 1980s, but unions saw the pressures for concessionary settlements as only the temporary products of difficult economic conditions and new competitive forces. They did, however, expect some permanency in what they might get in exchange for granting concessions—an expanded role in management decision-making and access to company financial records. Above all, union negotiators were realists; they understood there was a deep crisis that demanded nothing less than extraordinary sacrifices. But many were naturally reluctant to sacrifice past bargaining gains to keep employers afloat and demanded that they be treated in new ways—as legitimate workplace representatives and as partners in decision-making. And they expected that concessions would be rolled back once company performance improved, and that there would be equality of sacrifice on the part of managers (that is, managers would take similar cuts in their own compensation).

During the first wave of concession bargaining the employer's estimates of company's "ability to pay" dominated discussions at the bargaining table, and was no longer just another factor, like industry or community wage levels or the cost of living, to be debated. Settlements were custom-tailored to fit the special needs of the employer or individual plant rather than follow broader industrial patterns. Union negotiators were told there would have to be changes in work rules, so productivity could increase and unit labor costs fall simultaneously to a more competitive level.

[5] For example, a prominent textbook on collective bargaining (Katz and Kochan 2004, 457) defined concessionary bargaining as: "The negotiation of pay freezes, pay cuts, rollbacks, or work rules changes that occurred frequently in the 1980s." And Freeman (1986, 131) wrote "Many have dubbed the eighties (1980s) the era of the 'giveback' in collective bargaining."

The first wave of concession bargaining was a planned retreat, not a rout; it was the adaptation of conventional collective bargaining to severe economic conditions and competition (Rubenfeld 1983). Groundbreaking concessions were negotiated at companies facing strong competition, often for the first time, from low-cost nonunion firms. Concession bargaining became the norm for the larger and older airlines (the so-called "legacy carriers"), and the domestic automakers.

Concession bargaining ebbed with the economic recovery, but by then the unions had been seriously weakened. The new way to bargain was a shock to their system. Well-established patterns of industry or company-wide bargaining were suddenly broken. Management had become much more assertive in bargaining (Wever 1983). The mutual accommodation behind bargaining—the "labor accord" that we discuss later—was greatly weakened. To many employers it seemed only natural that if bargaining could be about taking steps forward in good times, it could also be about taking a few steps backward in hard times. The foundation was now in place for a second wave of concession bargaining—one that would fundamentally change how unions and employers deal with each other.

The Second Wave

Since the start of the twenty-first century, employers once again demanded concessions from unions (Chaison 2007). But now the assumptions and the conduct behind the concessions had radically changed. Employers demanded that wages and benefits be cut but they did not promise that jobs would be saved or that the concessions would be for one time only. The typical negotiation frequently morphed into a confrontational, one-sided meeting with the union simply being told that awful things (e.g., plants closings with job loss) would happen if it did not agree to concessions and that officers were obligated to sell concessions to the members. And once again, a few employers saw concession bargaining as a lucrative way to demand and receive concessions even if these were not warranted by the company's financial health (Schwartz 2010).

The first incidents of the new concession bargaining were at companies facing intense low-cost nonunion competition, either domestic or international—the Detroit automakers, the older airlines, auto parts makers, and other manufacturers. It spread to the city and state governments dealing with unsustainable labor costs and heavily unionized workforces. With ultra-concession bargaining, the balance of power had clearly shifted to management (Clark et al. 2002). There was now a new collective bargaining, and the tough, bitter negotiations at the Boston Globe did not seem so extraordinary after all.

References

Answers.com (2011) Concession bargaining. http://www.answers.com. Accessed 15 March 2011

Boston Globe could file shut down notice Monday (2009) http://www.reuters.com. 4 May. Accessed 4 May 2009.

Cappelli P (1983) Concession bargaining and the national economy. Proceedings of the 35th annual meeting of the Industrial Relations Research Association, 362–371.

Concessionary bargaining: Will the new cooperation last? (1982) Business Week, 14 June: 66–81.

Chaison G (2006) Unions in American. Cornell University Press, Ithaca NY.

Chaison G (2007) Airline negotiations and the new concessionary bargaining. J. of Lab Res 28: 643–657.

Clark et al. (2002) (eds). Collective bargaining in the private sector. University of Illinois, Industrial Relations Research Association, Champagne-Urbana Ill.

Freeman RB (1986) In search of wage concessions in standard data sets. Industrial Rel. 25: 131–145.

Gavin R (2009) Guaranteed jobs came at a price. Boston Globe 18 April: B4.

Gavin R, O'Brien K (2009) Hope builds for Globe, Guild deal. Boston Globe 6 May 2009:A1.

Henle P (1973) Reverse collective bargaining: A look at some concession situations. Ind. and Labor Relat. Rev. 26: 956–978.

Katz HC, Kochan TA (2004) Introduction to collective bargaining and industrial relations. McGraw-Hill Irwin, Boston MA.

Kurtz H (2009) New York Times backs off closure of Boston Globe. Washington Post 5 May 2009:C1.

Lewin et al. (2011) Getting it right: Empirical evidence and policy implications from research on public sector unionism and collective bargaining. Employment policy and research network. http://www.lera.org 16 March. Accessed 20 March 2011.

Marks A (2009) What's next for Boston Globe: wage cuts or renewed bargaining? Christian Science Monitor. http://www.CSMonitor.com 9 June. Accessed 29 February 2012.

Miner T (1982) Concessionary bargaining. Chicago-Kent Law Rev. 59: 981–996.

Mitchell DJB (1985) Concessionary bargaining and wage determination. Bus. Econ. 7: 45–50.

O'Brien K (2009) Times Company seeks Globe bids. Boston Globe 10 June, 2009: A1.

Perez-Pena R (2009a) New York Times Co. decides not to sell Boston Globe. New York Times http://www.dealbook.nytimes.com 14 October. Accessed 7 July, 2011.

Perez-Pena R (2009b) Tentative settlement at the Boston Globe. New York Times 24 June: 1.

Perez-Pena R (2009c) Times Co. said to be considering closing Boston Globe. New York Times. 4 April: 5.

Rubenfeld S (1983) Today's contract concession: Tomorrow's impact. Working paper 83–6, Department of Business Administration, University Minnesota, Duluth.

Ross C (2011) Businessman prepares bid to buy Globe. http://www.Boston.com 12 May. Accessed 12 May 2011.

Schwartz ND (2010) Industries find surging profits in deeper cuts. New York Times. 25 June: A1.

USlegal.com (2011) Concession bargaining law and legal definition. http://www.uslegal.com Accessed 1 July 2011.

What next for the Boston Globe? (2009) http://www.csmonitor.com 7 June. Accessed 9 June 2011.

Wever K (1983) Concession bargaining—1979–1983: Not just the same old thing. Working paper WP1478-83a, Sloan School of Management. Massachusetts Institute of Technology.

Chapter 2
The World of Concession Bargaining

Abstract Concession bargaining is the mirror image of conventional collective bargaining as employers act and unions react, rather than the reverse. Concession bargaining is shaped more by the employer's ability to pay than by the other factors brought up at the bargaining table such as changes in the cost of living or labor productivity. The basic assumptions of concession bargaining are employer credibility (that employers have made credible cases of hardship); the *quid pro quo* (that the union gets something (usually job security) in return for what it gives (usually lower wages and benefits)); and a sense of "for this time only" (that concessions are made only once and not repeated). Concession bargaining is discussed in terms of wage freezes and cuts, two-tiered wage systems, the duration of collective bargaining agreements, health care benefits, pensions, and work rules.

Keywords Concession bargaining • Conventional collective bargaining • Two-tiered wages • Defined benefit pensions • Defined contributions pensions • Contract duration • Health care benefits • Work rules • Voluntary employee beneficiary associations

Concession bargaining is, in many ways, a mirror image of conventional collective bargaining.[1] In the world of concession bargaining, employers act and unions react, the reverse of what happens in conventional collective bargaining. To save their members' jobs, unions take steps backward rather than forward, giving up past gains instead of making new ones. The final settlement at the bargaining table is shaped mostly by the employers' ability to pay (as argued by the employer) rather than by the usual factors for evaluating demand and offers, such as increases in productivity,

[1] For brief reviews of the essentials of concession bargaining see Henle (1973), Miner (1982), or Alvarez (2010).

G. Chaison, *The New Collective Bargaining*, SpringerBriefs in Economics,
DOI 10.1007/978-1-4614-4024-6_2, © Springer Science+Business Media New York 2012

the rising cost of living, or comparable wages paid elsewhere. Wage-setting formulas, including traditional annual wage adjustments, which had set the tone of negotiations, are suddenly disregarded by companies claiming they cannot afford whatever might have been acceptable in the past. Bargaining patterns that establish one collective agreement as the model for others in the region or the industry are much less controlling because employers challenge their relevancy (Freedman and Fullmer 1982; Nay 1991). Once powerful comparisons in bargaining between settlements (who got what?) and over time (what was given in the past?) mean little to employers who plea they should only have to pay a hardship wage—a wage that fits their present circumstances.

Under concession bargaining, unions are reluctant to strike because they could possibly drive weak employers out of business or force the hand of employers who have threatened to close plants and send work abroad. When strikes do occur, they are abbreviated affairs, lasting only a few hours or a day or two. Strikes signal the workers' frustration with the lack of progress in bargaining or demonstrate the union officers' intent to do all they can to get a deal; they are no longer tests of endurance used to pry settlements from reluctant employers. Also, unions can no longer rely on pattern bargaining—they lose their leveraging tactic of striking one company, getting a good collective agreement, and then imposing its terms on other companies in the industry. Companies resist traditional bargaining patterns, and even incite and withstand a strike to buttress their argument that they must pay less, not the same, as their competitors in order to survive (Freedman and Fullmer 1982; Chaison 2006). Without the ability to launch a lasting strike, or at least threaten one credibly, unions cannot resist employers' demands for concessions. Moreover, in concession bargaining, unions cannot count on community support during a strike because they appear obstinate and short-sighted by putting higher wages above saving jobs (Craft et al. 1985).

Collective agreements must be ratified by union members. In contract ratification following concession bargaining, when members vote "yea" or "nay" on tentative agreements, nothing can be taken for granted. Members might reject an agreement strongly endorsed by their bargaining committee if they feel bargainers could have and should have done better. Or they might accept an agreement but by a close vote as a way to signal to their union's officers that they deserve more but they are willing to accept the terms of the agreement, albeit reluctantly. For contract ratification, union members must accept the notion that the settlement is the best their union could do under the circumstances and that now is not the time for a prolonged fight but the time for sacrifices to save jobs. A fight can come later when the contract is renegotiated. Much of what is given up in bargaining today can be recouped in bargaining in better times. Union leaders must be willing to argue that without a settlement, even an admittedly poor one, all will be lost and the company might go under. They must present the concession agreement as a sort of placeholder; it keeps workers on their jobs and the union as bargaining agent—both big accomplishments in hard times—even if the contract terms are unattractive.

The outcomes of concession bargaining are matters of faith. For union members to ratify collective agreements with concessions, they must have faith in the need for concessions, the payoff of concessions, and the this-time-only character of the sacrifices they make.

The Assumptions Underlying Concession Bargaining

There are three assumptions by workers and their unions that are crucial to concession bargaining: (1) concessions must be based on credible employer claims of hardship; (2) concessions must have a *quid pro quo* with workers receiving something of value for what they give up; and (3) concessions must be seen as for one time only and not something to be asked for again. (In a later chapter I argue that under the new variant of concession bargaining—ultra-concession bargaining—employers ignore these assumptions.)

Employer Credibility. First and foremost, union members must believe that employers are making credible cases of hardship. They must see companies as being in dire straits, with limited options, and their survival hanging in the balance.[2] All would be lost, bankruptcy would be declared, and plants would be closed, unless there are cuts in labor costs (Henle 1973; Miner 1982).[3] Also, it must be shown that the times are so dark that there will be equality of sacrifice—managers will share in the suffering and accept roughly similar concessions to those negotiated by the workforce. When workers' wages are cut, managers cannot get raises.

Management must be willing to provide unions with financial data, once considered strictly confidential, necessary to support their claims of hardship. Otherwise, their credibility will be damaged and concessions will seem unjustified. As a news reporter observed during the wave of concession bargaining in the 1980s: "In return

[2] For example, in a case discussed later, there was criticism of a company that demanded concessions without the proper justification. Workers walked out in a strike at the Mott's apple juice plant in upstate New York after the company demanded a $1.50 wage cut and a freeze in pensions, not because the company was doing poorly (actually it was profitable) but because the company simply felt that less was being paid in the area and that its compensation costs should be brought in line. The company claimed that it only wanted to be more profitable (Greenhouse 2010).

See Bell (1995) for a discussion of the strong links between individual firm performance and negotiated concessions—concessions were less likely in firms with above average performance.

[3] Bunkley (2010a) wrote that UAW Local 1112 in Lordstown, Ohio had a reputation as a militant union opposing concessions negotiated by their national union with General Motors in the 1980s; but it approved a contract granting major concessions in work rules in 2008. Apparently, members of the local became less hostile to concessions when they saw the damage that foreign competition did to the financial health of their employer and the possibility that GM would soon be bankrupt. Job security became their highest union concern because the company had made a credible case of hardship (Bunkley 2010a, b).

for concessions ... unions are demanding a look at company books to certify that financial ruin is imminent. Reluctantly, many firms are going along." (Lanoutte 1982, 425)

Credibility also means that employers should state their intent to use the savings from concessions to invest in creating and saving jobs. For example, U.S. Steel received tremendous criticism in the 1980s when it demanded concessions during bargaining and then proceeded to buy the Marathon Oil Company (Davis 1984). And workers striking Verizon in 2011 complained that the company's demands for pension, health care plan, and work rule concessions were unjustified. Verizon's landline division, which employed the strikers, was less profitable than its wireless division, but still made money, and overall the company had an operating income of $9 billion in the first half of 2011. Verizon, like U.S. Steel, simply could not make a believable case why it needed concessions (Greenhouse 2011a, c).

The *Quid Pro Quo*. Union members must be able to assume that there will be a *quid pro quo* (*this for that*) in concession bargaining (Kelber 2011).[4] There must be some give and take with the union gaining something roughly equal in value to what it has given up. In other words, the union and its members must believe that they are getting something in return for agreeing to concessions.[5] Perhaps jobs that might have been lost will now be saved. Some plants scheduled for closing might remain open and even renovated to make new models or product lines.

Employee sacrifices might be matched with employer agreement to allow for greater union influence. There might even be a union seat on the board of directors with the right to debate and vote on strategy issues like new products and plant relocation (Plovnick and Chaison 1985; Chaison and Plovnick 1986). Union concessions have been shown to prompt cooperative plans ranging from quality circles to quality-of-work-life programs—both are structured programs that attempt to increase productivity and quality by eliciting worker and union participation in decision-making (Chaison and Plovnick 1986). What happens in concession bargaining is that "employers [take] things away from unions while at the same time offering unions some of the very things they had always wanted" (Katz et al. 2008, 42).

For This Time Only. To be acceptable to union negotiators and members, concessions must be seen as unique, extraordinary measures that are agreed to only once and not repeated. There should be an explicit sense of singularity in an employer's

[4] Cappelli (1985, 91) saw the exchange relationship as a key facet of concession bargaining and concluded that "unions may moderate labor costs through concession bargaining if jobs are threatened and if such moderation is likely to generate a clear improvement in employment security." For a description of trade-offs during concession bargaining see Bureau of National Affairs (1982).

[5] In their study of the workers' approval or rejection of collective agreements with concessions (wage freezes, the elimination of a traditional wage increase, postponement of cost of living allowances, and the elimination of all personal holidays) negotiated between the UAW and General motors, Kaufman and Martinez-Vazquez (1988) found that workers in plants with large layoffs voted in favor of the concessions only if they believed that concessions would save their jobs.

demand—one single demand for concessions is enough and if fully granted there will be no need to repeat it. If members agree to concessions, the company's difficulties will assumedly end. The storm will pass and normalcy will return. Future demands for concessions will not be needed.

If the concession bargaining of the 1980s (the first wave, to be discussed in the next chapter) taught us anything it is that union members are willing to make extraordinary sacrifices and support collective agreements that are radical breaks with the past if, and only if, they believe they are doing something that can be justified economically. Union members will reject a core principle of unionism—that bargaining is forward-moving by adding to prior agreements rather than subtracting from them.

Common Concessions

Wage Freezes and Cuts. The most frequently negotiated concessions are wage freezes—agreements to have wages remain unchanged for the duration of the collective agreement or, more commonly, for wages remain unchanged for the first year or two of the agreement.[6] These are frequently offset by lump-sum payments—a single bonus payment to workers (Bell 1989). They are also called signing bonuses or ratification bonuses, and may be for a specific amount ($500, $750, and $1,000 are most common[7]) or a percent of pay (1, 3, 4, or 7 % of base pay are most common) (Bureau of National Affairs 2010). Employers prefer to give a lump-sum payment, if they give anything, because it is not added to the base pay rate used to calculate overtime pay and employer contributions to pensions and health care plans. Employers also understand how collective bargaining agreements compound each other—they build on each other year after year so that next year's wage increase compounds this year's increase. This does not happen with lump-sum payments. If, for example, a worker earns $40,000 per year and receives a 3 % wage increase at the end of a 2-year agreement, then wages will go up to $41,200 ($40,000 + $1,200 [3 % × $40,000]). But if there is a $1,200 lump-sum payment when the agreement is signed, the base wage at the *end* of the agreement will remain at $40,000, and future raises will be based on that figure.

[6] In his review of concessionary settlements, Alvarez (2010) found that slightly more than half of bargaining unions agreed to wage and benefit reductions, and slightly less than half agreed to wage and benefits freezes.

[7] For example, one collective agreement described in the BNA's database Collective Bargaining Agreement Settlements in October 2005 was a 4-year agreement in manufacturing with no salary increase but with a $6,000 signing bonus. In contrast, another agreement in manufacturing signed 2 years earlier was for 3 years with no wage increase for the first and second year, a 15 cents per hour raise in the last year, and a $300 signing bonus.

The Bureau of National Affairs (BNA), a private labor relations research organization in Washington D.C., maintains a database of collective bargaining settlements. From 2000 to 2010, there were 7,560 settlements recorded in the database. Eighteen percent of these had some sort of wage freeze and 16 % had lump-sum payments. Only 2 % of the settlements had complete freezes, that is, wages freezes without any partially offsetting lump-sum payments (Bureau of National Affairs 2010)

There are a number of ways to cut wages and these can be even more nuanced than wage freezes. Wages can be cut at the start of an agreement, in steps over time, (e.g., down by 3 % each year for a 3-year agreement) or at the expiration of the collective agreement so the workers do not feel the cuts for the duration of the agreement they are asked to ratify. Wages can also be cut by eliminating, reducing, capping (setting a limit on), deferring, or suspending COLAs (Cost of Living Allowances, which are automatic, periodic wage increases based on increases in measures of price changes, usually the Consumer Price Index). Less than a quarter of workers covered by collective agreements have COLA clauses (Ragan and Bratsberg 2000). In a commonly negotiated concession, all COLA payments may be frozen until the next agreement.

Two-Tier Wages. Two-tier wage systems are clauses in collective bargaining agreements that stipulate that new workers will be hired for less than present workers doing the same jobs.[8] Wages for the lower-tier workers are often 20 or 30 % less than those of higher-tier workers (Chaison 2009). Or the workers on the lower tier might receive lesser benefits—for example, their health care plans might be made more expensive or provide less coverage than that of higher-tier workers. Lower-tier workers might also have weaker protections against layoffs.[9] When the present workers ratify collective agreements establishing two-tiered plans, they are essentially deciding that future hires (members not yet present to vote on the agreement) will receive less than they do. They ask others to sacrifice so their own jobs will be more secure.

In the BNA database for 2000–2010, two-tiered wage plans were in collective bargaining agreements of such diverse employers as a large state-wide health insurance company, a motorcycle manufacturer, a small mid-western city, a poultry processor, an auto parts maker, a television station, and a city newspaper, among others (Bureau of National Affairs 2010).

---

[8] For reviews of two-tier wage systems see Heetderks and Martin (1991), Salpukas (1985, 1987), Thomas and Kleiner (1992), Two-tier wage discrimination and the duty of fair representation (1985), Uchitelle (2006, 2010), Chaison (2009), and Lee (2011).

[9] For example, in 2003, a collective agreement was ratified at Verizon that provided a lump-sum payment instead of a wage increase in the first year of a 5-year agreement, 2 % wage increases for each of the next 4 years, and, for the entire agreement, protections against layoffs and involuntary transfers for *present* workers but not for *newly hired* workers (the lower-tier workers) (Greenhouse 2003).

Unions have been sharply criticized by labor activists as well as their own members for agreeing to two-tiered wages because they create a group of second-class workers and violate the time-honored union principle of "equal pay for equal work" or pay uniformity across workers (Jacobs 2009). Two-tiered wages may negatively affect union organizing by convincing nonunion workers that the labor movement is dominated by older, senior members and officers who would be willing to sacrifice their younger and new hire's interests in favor of the interests of an older generation (Bell 1989; Chaison 2009; Two-tier wage discrimination and the duty of fair representation 1985). But some union leaders promote two-tier systems as the only way to avoid plant closings and eventual wage cuts for all, and encourage employers to hire more workers (e.g., Naughton and Green 2010). They argue that either a few new workers must have lower paying jobs or all workers could lose their jobs. And, they add, a single unified tier will be negotiated as soon as possible. Two tiers will become one.

Some employers are hesitant to propose two-tiered systems because they worry about lowering new employees' incentive to work and causing them to be so dissatisfied with their relative pay that they leave to find jobs elsewhere. But other employers argue that imposing a second lower tier is the only way to cut labor costs and survive low wage compensation. Two-tier systems, they claim, will add value to the firm by reducing the overall wage bill and making the company more competitive against the low-cost nonunion firms in the industry (Thomas and Kleiner 1992). In industries where there are high turnover, such as retailing, most workers will soon be in the lower tier, so when a union agrees to a two-tier system it might be the same effect as cutting wages (Chaison 2009). Moreover, as Jacobs (2009) observed, in future bargaining the unions' priorities shift toward raising the lower-tier wages and the wages on the higher tier receive little increase if any.

Some variations of two-tiered wage systems are shown in Fig. 2.1. At the time of the signing of a 3-year collective agreement (time 0) two tiers are created—the higher *A* and the lower *B*. The higher-tier workers (the present workers) accept a wage freeze and are paid $25 per hour for the duration of the agreement (line *A*). Those on the lower tier, line *B*, will receive $15 per hour for doing the same work as workers on A. If this arrangement is temporary; the wages of tier B workers can either rise in annual steps (line *Bx*) or fold into the higher tier at the expiration of the agreement (line *By*). If there is a permanent two-tiered plan, the lower tier (*B*) would continue unchanged.

There are other possibilities, not shown in Fig. 2.1, which can reduce the impact of two-tier wage settlements. There might be buy-downs—payments at the start of the collective agreement to damper the impact of the two-tier system. Lump-sum payments as buy-downs may have the effect of delaying two-tier systems—the lower-tier workers get a lump-sum payment for the duration of the agreement and the lower tier might not be established until the end of the agreement. There can also be restrictions on lower tiers; for example, some but not all of the newly hired workers (e.g., only those performing specified crafts) will be assigned in the lower tier. There might be lower tiers for employee benefits rather than wages; for example, there is a lower tier only for pensions but not for wages (all workers doing the

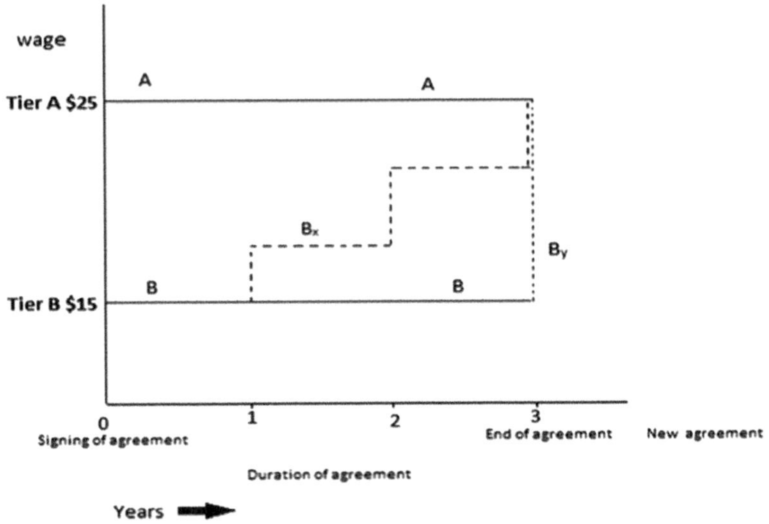

Fig. 2.1 Two-tiered wage systems

same job receive the same pay, but higher-tier workers receive their usual defined benefits pension plans (discussed later) while new hires receive less predictable defined contribution plans). Or it may take longer for lower-tier workers to receive the same pension as higher-tier workers.[10] This might be more acceptable to members reluctant to approve permanent two-tiered wages. However, once it is agreed to, the basic objective of the two-tier systems remains the same—workers have voted in their own self-interest to disadvantage those not yet hired and without a voice in the matter.

Looking at the BNA's survey of expiring collective bargaining agreements in 2010, we find that one-third of agreements had two-tier wages (Bureau of National Affairs 2010). They were agreed to by employers and unions at such large and diverse companies as Harley-Davidson, Ford Motor Company, Tyson Foods, Bank of America, and PPG Industries, as well as community colleges, city transit systems, community public service departments, and health insurers.

Longer (or Shorter) Collective Bargaining Agreements. Collective bargaining agreements have clauses, usually at their end, that state their duration. Often, when a collective bargaining is due to expire, either party—the union or management—must notify the other of its intent to renegotiate the agreement; the terms of the collective agreement will then continue until a new agreement is signed or an

[10] For example, in a bargaining proposal for county deputy sheriffs in California, newly hired workers (the lower tier) would have to work 5 more years than regular workers (the higher-tier workers) to receive maximum retirement benefits (Edwards 2010).

impasse is reached in bargaining.[11] An alternative, but less common approach, is to have the agreement simply expire on a certain date; before it expires the parties must negotiate a new one.[12] In either case, the average duration of a collective agreement is about 3 years (Chaison 2006).

When concessions are negotiated, employers may try to "lock them in" by demanding longer collective agreements. They will claim they need greater certainty of lower labor costs or stability of labor relations so they can plan for the future. They will also argue that they will keep some plants open that might otherwise be closed if they have a long-term commitment from the union to lower operating costs. In other words, jobs can be saved, but only with longer collective agreements.

Some employers, however, may try to have it both ways. In bargaining, they will plea that they need a long agreement to lock-in savings from concessions. But after a year or two, they will argue that they need to reopen the agreement for more negotiations and further concessions.[13] They might pressure unions to reopen certain parts of the collective agreements, for example, the clauses on wages or health care benefits, claiming that what they agreed to in the past does not reflect changes in the competitive position of the company and its need for cost reductions.

Health Care Benefits. Health care plans are frequently the most expensive employee benefits to cut in concession bargaining. Coverage under health care insurance plans is greater among unionized workers (78 %) than nonunion workers (51 %) (U.S. Bureau of Labor Statistics 2009) although this might change if workers are required to have health care insurance coverage under federal or state legislation.

---

[11] For example, in the collective bargaining agreement between the National Association of Letter Carriers and the U.S. Postal Service for 2006–2011, the section on duration reads "Unless otherwise provided, this agreement shall be effective November 1, 2006 and shall remain in force and effect to and including 12 midnight November 20, 2011, and unless either party desires to terminate or modify it, for successive annual periods. The party demanding such termination or modification must serve written notice of such intent to the other party not less than 90 days or more than 120 days before the expiration of the Agreement" (National Association of Letter Carriers 2006, Sect. 2.2).

In the industries covered by the Railway Labor Act of 1926 (the railroads and the airlines) collective agreements do not have fixed expiration dates, but rather they have amenable dates. After the amendable date, the contract remains in force until a new agreement is reached (Nordenflycht and Kochan 2003).

[12] For example, the basic collective agreement of the Major League Baseball Players Association for 2007–2011 has a clause that simply states "The agreement shall terminate on December 30, 2011" (Major League Baseball Players Association 2007, Article XXVI).

[13] Alternatively, a wage reopener may be negotiated and become part of the initial settlement. For example, one agreement in the BNA's database was for 5 years, with a 4 % increase in the first, second, and third years with the contract then to be reopened for wage negotiations after another year. Another agreement for 4 years had wage increases in the first 3 years and was reopened for the negotiations of both wages and benefits in the last year (Bureau of National Affairs 2010).

Health care benefits are so expensive that it is only natural that they would be an important issue in concession bargaining. In negotiations, employers place intense pressure on unions, often by threats of mass layoffs, to reduce the costs of health care benefits paid to unionized workers.

Concession bargaining over health care benefits usually proceeds along one of three paths:

- Cutting benefits—reducing the benefits offered under plans or limiting who is covered under plans (e.g., by reducing the coverage of retirees or workers' family members).
- Cost-shifting—requiring that workers pay more under their health insurance (e.g., substituting a $200 deductible for a $100 deductible, or increasing employee co-payments to family dental insurance).
- Off-loading health care benefits—devising and paying for arrangements under which organizations or committees serve as trusts to administer and pay for health care insurance plans.

The first option, lowering costs by weakening plans, is the most obvious and easiest approach. The deductible amount may simply be increased so that workers have less first-dollar coverage (i.e., they have to pay more up-front for services) or some options may be excluded from coverage. Employers may demand that more prescription medications have to be paid for by workers. They can exclude dental work, or eye exams and eye glasses. Or they may negotiate higher payments for family members may be increased and their coverage weakened.

Meeting union resistance to weakening plans, employers might insist that employees pay a larger share of the premium for health care benefits. Negotiations can be about how much of a plan is paid for by workers (e.g., increasing the workers' share of the annual fee from 20 to 30 %). If there are a large number of workers covered, even small changes in cost-sharing can bring about savings of millions of dollars (Bradbury and Chaison 1987). An option that is strongly resisted by unions and their members is the first time employee contribution to plans because they see this as opening the door to future cost-shifting. Workers might have become accustomed to never paying for health care benefits—first time payments may seem like violation of a sacred job right.

An employer may also cut health care costs by negotiating VEBAs (Voluntary Employee Beneficiary Associations)—agreements to transfer the obligation to provide health care benefits for retirees to unions. Unions administer the VEBA trust funds and employers pay a fraction of the costs of benefits (say 60 or 70 %) to start the fund.[14] VEBAs can also be paid for by combinations of the workers' deferred wage increases (workers accepting a lower wage if the savings fund the VEBA), and the employers' payment of cash or company stock (which is backed by financial instruments under which employers agree to pay if the price of the company's stock

[14] For reviews of VEBAs see Wallach (2003), Davolt (2006), and Kutalik (2007).

set aside for the VEBA falls below a specified amount) (e.g., United Automobile Workers 2009).

From the perspective of employers, VEBAs are valuable for off-loading costly health care benefits, but from the unions' perspective VEBAs are bargaining concessions that carry new obligations and risks. Unions try to negotiate VEBAs that are sufficiently funded to provide lifetime funding for current and future retirees. Historically, VEBAs were promoted by unions in the 1920s as a way to create trusts that would insure that workers receive the health care benefits to which they were entitled, but now VEBAs are most often used to cut the costs of health care benefits for retirees by having someone other than employers deal with them.

VEBAs can benefit employers and present workers as well as retirees. They can reduce the employers' liabilities on the company balance sheets, thus making the company look healthier financially, improving its bond rating, and saving money they otherwise would have used to service bond offerings. For the retired workers, VEBAs mean that health care benefits are protected; health care plans in VEBAs are separated from the company and cannot be cut by creditors if the employer eventually declares bankruptcy. Another advantage of VEBAs is that they are tax deductible for employers—they can grow on a tax deferred basis and there are no tax penalties for early distributions.

But union negotiators also understand how VEBAs can create conflicts of interest situations for unions. Acting as VEBA trustees, unions might someday have to agree to reduce the health care benefits of their own retired members. When VEBAs are funded largely through company stock, unions would be concerned that their strikes or bargaining settlements might reduce the value of that stock. Unions would also be concerned about the public impression that they now own the company and are responsible for its success, exaggerated as this claim is (Austen 2010). More will be said about VEBAs in Chap. 4 when we discuss concession bargaining in the automobile industry.

Pensions. In concession bargaining, employers try to negotiate cost savings through changes in pension plans. Employee pension plans are not required by law, but they are common among unionized workers (80 % have them) and nonunion workers (51 %) (U.S. Bureau of Labor Statistics 2009). *Defined benefit* pension plans guarantee a fixed monthly stipend for each retiree's lifetime and they are usually more costly to employers. In contrast, *defined contribution* plans (also called *cash balance plans*) set up personal investment accounts and does not guarantee the amount of the eventual pay-off. Thus, they are less risky and expensive to employers but then they are less valuable to employees (Greenhouse 2011b). Unionized workers more often have defined benefits plans (68 %) compared to nonunion workers (14 %) (Furchgott-Roth 2008).[15]

[15] For the advantages and disadvantages of defined contribution and defined benefit pension plans see Lewin et al. (2011, 11–12).

Nearly half of the cost of all workers employment benefits is devoted to pensions. Employers commonly consider pensions to be a financial drain, because they are paid to workers who no longer produce anything. In the public sector, employer contributions to pension plans are considered too costly by communities facing budget deficits and a fertile area for concession bargaining (Walsh 2011). But workers and their unions see pensions as deferred wage increases and argue that they had accepted lower wages in the past so their employers could contribute to pension plans that pay them in the future when they retire.

In concession bargaining, employers try to modify, freeze, or terminate pension plans. Employers press unions to agree to changes in pension plans substituting a less expensive option for a more expensive one (e.g., convert a defined benefit plan into a defined contribution plan). They can also modify plans by delaying payments or by requiring workers to accumulate more years on the job before earning maximum retirement benefits.[16] Employers can bargain to modify the payment formula (e.g., if the formula states that workers can retire at the age of 50 to earn 3 % of their highest annual pay multiplied by the number of years they worked, the employer can insist that the age of retirement be changed to 55 or 60) (Furchgott-Roth 2008). Also, employers can insist on a two-tier pension plan—the present workers' pension arrangement remaining unchanged, but new workers—the lower-tier workers—receive a pension for which they get less or pay more.[17]

During negotiations an employer can pressure a union to terminate a pension plan or to freeze it by not adding further to it. If a plan is terminated or abandoned by the company, a federal agency (the Pension Benefit Guarantee Corporation or the PBGC) will administer the plan and guarantee the retirees a payment, though usually an amount that is less than what they would have otherwise received.

Work Rules. Employers negotiate for work rule concessions with two objectives in mind—improving productivity and reducing costs. The employers' demands to unions would include:

- Expanding jobs so that workers can perform outside of their normal job classifications; this might be done by decreasing the size and composition of work crews.
- Changing layoff policies so that it is easier for employers to adjust the size of the workforce and use performance rather than seniority as the basis for determining who goes and who stays.
- Permitting management to contract out work to workers of other companies (e.g., for food services, security, and maintenance).

---

[16] An analysis of employer attempts to control the growth of pensions found that the most common employer approach was to change the basis for calculating a pension, for example moving from a 3-year average of an employees' highest salary to a 5-year average (Phaneuf 2011).

[17] Jacobs (2009) called two-tiered pension plans "soft freezes" when plans are frozen for lower-tier workers while contributions continue for higher-tier workers. In contrast, "hard freezes" end contributions for all employees.

- Introducing new production technologies more readily by setting new rules for dealing with issues surrounding that technology, for example, who will use the new technology, who will repair and install the new technology, and how increased production will be reflected in workers' compensation.
- Ending restrictions on hiring part-time workers so part-timers can be used as replacements for full-time workers who miss a shift for unforeseen reasons, thus reducing the overtime paid for replacements.
- Relaxing regulations on who may bid on jobs and who can be hired, thereby alleviating the need to fill vacancies with new workers rather than through transfers or promotions.
- Eliminating or restricting job protection plans that guarantee continued income for workers who are laid off.
- Rearranging workers' time schedules to eliminate hours when workers are clocked in and getting paid but not working.

Unions will resist changes in work rules that cause jobs to be cut, lessen union control over who does what work, or result in fewer opportunities for promotions. The measure and application of seniority, a key element of work rules, can be highly valued to unions and unionized workers. Accumulated seniority usually determines who gets to bid on the best jobs, who avoids layoffs, who has the right to transfer to other jobs, and, for workers in global firms, whose job will be protected from being transferred overseas. Unions support seniority plans because they are objective and easily understood and accepted by workers, though employers claim that seniority simply creates a protected group of older workers while discouraging younger workers and stinting their efforts.

Concession Bargaining and Conventional Bargaining

We should always keep in mind that concession bargaining occurs concurrently with conventional bargaining in our economy. One approach to bargaining may overshadow but not preclude the other, and even in times of intense concession bargaining, some bargaining situations might remain conventional. There will always be instances when unions and management prefer to bargain as they always have. But there have been two periods when union–management relations were dominated by concession bargaining. In the following chapters we examine the two waves of concession bargaining—the first in the 1980s when the core assumptions inherent in concession bargaining were still being respected, and the second occurring since the start of this century, when core assumptions were largely disregarded and concession bargaining reached a new level of intensity and vindictiveness. In a concluding chapter we explore the broad implications of the new concession bargaining.

References

Alvarez R (2010) Do concessions work? (Part I) http://www.thefreelibrary.com Accessed 17 March 2010.

Austen B (2010) Who's the boss? The Atlantic http://www.theatlantic.com 14 May. Accessed 14 May, 2010

Bell LA (1989) Union concessions in the 1980s. Fed. Reserve Board of N. Y. Q. Rev. Summer: 44–58.

Bell LA (1995) Wage concessions in the 1980s: The importance of firm-specific factors. Ind. and Labor Relat. Rev. 48: 258–275.

Bradbury RC, Chaison GN (1987) Local union support for health care cost containment. New England J. of Hum. Serv. 7:25–29.

Bunkley N (2010a) Auto union curbs its anger to survive: Once militant workers choose to compromise rather than see jobs die. Intl. Herald Tribune. 17 January. Accessed 30 March 2011.

Bunkley N (2010b) UAW wants to share in Big-3's gains after years of pain. New York Times 12 May 13: B1.

Bureau of National Affairs (1982) Labor relations in an economic recession: Job losses and concession bargaining. Bureau of National Affairs: Washington D.C.

Bureau of National Affairs (2010) Collective bargaining settlement database. BNA, Washington DC

Cappelli P (1985) Plant level concession bargaining. Ind. Labor Relat. Rev. 39: 90–104.

Chaison G (2006) Unions in America. Sage, Thousand Oaks, CA.

Chaison G (2009) Two-tier wage settlements and the legitimacy of American unions Proceedings of the fifteenth congress of the International Industrial Relations Association. Sydney, Australia

Chaison, G, Plovnick M (1986) Is there a new collective bargaining? Calif. Manag. Review 28:54–61.

Craft JA et al. (1985) Concession bargaining and unions: Impacts and implications. J. Lab. Res. 6:167–179.

Davis WM (1984) Collective bargaining in 1983: A crowded agenda. Mon. Labor Rev. 106: 3–16.

Davolt S (2006) Viva la VEBA benefit trust ready for a comeback. Employee Benefits News 1 January.

Edwards A (2010) San Bernadino County, cities seek pension concessions http://www.sbsun.com 24 May. Accessed 25 May 2011.

Freedman A, Fullmer WJ (1982) Last rites for pattern bargaining. Harvard Bus. Rev. 60:30–48

Furchgott-Roth D (2008) Union vs. private pension plans: How secure are union members' retirements. Hudson Institute Report, Hudson Institute, Washington D.C.

Greenhouse S (2003) Verizon and unions agree on tentative 5-year contract. New York Times 5 September 5: C1,C6.

Greenhouse S (2010) In the Mott's strike, more than pay at stake. New York Times http://www.nytimes.com 18 August. Accessed 18 August 2010.

Greenhouse (2011a) Citing stalemate, Verizon workers strike. New York Times. 6 August. Accessed 20 October 2011.

Greenhouse S (2011b) Pensions on the move. New York Times 1 March: 1

Greenhouse S (2011c) Verizon landline unit at heart of strike. New York Times, http://www.nytimes.com 10 August. Accessed 10 August 2011.

Heetderks TD, Martin JE (1991) Employee perceptions of the effects of a two-tier wage structures. J Labor Res 12:279–293.

Henle P (1973) Reverse collective bargaining? A look at some concession situations. Ind and Labor Relat. Rev. 26: 956–978.

Jacobs K (2009) A tale of two-tiers: Dividing workers in the age of neoliberalism. New Labor Forum 18: 67–77.

Katz HC et al. (2008) An introduction to collective bargaining and industrial relations. McGraw-Hill, New York.

Kaufman B, Martinez-Vazquez J (1988) Voting for wage concessions; The case of the 1982 GM-UAW negotiations. Indust. and Lab. Rel. Rev. 41: 183–194.

Kelber H (2011) Unions sacrifice wages and benefits to avoid massive layoffs of members. The Labor Educator. http://www.laboreducator.org. 22 July. Accessed 15 January 2012.

Kutalik C (2007) Automakers push health care trust solution for industry crisis. http://www.counterpunch.com 31 August. Accessed 31 August 2011.

Lanoutte WJ (1982) Recession brings labor, management closer on union contracts. National J. 6 March: 422–425.

Lee D (2011) Two-tier pay system brings reopening of GM plant, reviving hope. http://www.latimes.com 18 December. Accessed 18 December 2011.

Lewin et al. (2011) Getting it right: Empirical evidence and policy implications from research on public-sector unionism and collective bargaining. http://www.lera.org 16 March. Accessed 29 March 2011.

Major League Baseball Players Associations (2007) Collective bargaining agreement http://www.mlbpa.org. Accessed 10 March 2011.

Miner T (1982) Concession bargaining. Chicago-Kent Law Rev. 59: 981–996.

National Association of Letter Carriers (2006) Collective bargaining agreement with United States Postal Service. http://www.nalc.org 22 January. Accessed 15 August 2011.

Naughton K, Green J (2010) Ford investing $600 million, hiring 1,800 at SUV plant. http://www.bloomberg.com Accessed 9 December 2011.

Nay LA (1991) The determinants of concession bargaining in airline industry. Ind. Lab. Relat. Rev. 44: 307–323.

Nordenflycht A, Kochan TA (2003) Labor contract negotiations in the airline industry. Mon. Labor Rev. 126: 18–28.

Phaneuf KM (2011). Report: Connecticut lags in tackling retirement benefit costs. The Connecticut Mirror http://www.ctmirror.org 7 February. Accessed 12 August 2011.

Plovnick M, Chaison GN (1985) The relationship between concession bargaining and labor-management cooperation. Acad. Manag. J. 28: 697–704

Ragan JF, Bratsberg B (2000) UNICOLA: Why have cost-of-living clauses disappeared from union contracts and will they return? Southern Economic J. 67: 304–324.

Salpukas A (1985) The two-tier wage impact. New York Times October 30:1

Salpukas A (1987) Two-tier was system: For many it leads to a second class status. New York Times 21 July: 1

Thomas SL, Kleiner MM (1992) The effect of two-tier collective bargaining agreements on shareholder equity. Ind. Labor Relat. Rev. 45: 339–351.

Two-tier wage discrimination and the duty of fair representation (1985) Harvard Law Rev. 98: 631–649.

Uchitelle L (2006) Two tiers, slipping into one. New York Times http://www.nytimes.com 26 February. Accessed 1 August 2011

Uchitelle L (2010) Unions yield on wage scales to preserve jobs. http://www.nytimes.com 20 November. Accessed 12 August 2011.

United Auto Workers (2009) UAW-Ford modifications to 2007 agreement and addendum to VEBA agreement. http://www.uaw.org 24 February. Accessed 1 March 2009.

United States Bureau of Labor Statistics (2009) National compensation survey, employee benefits in the United States. United States Department of Labor, Washington D.C.

Wallach L (2003) Benefits of forming a voluntary employee beneficiary association. The CPA Journal http://www.nycpa.org. 1 September. Accessed 12 August 2011.

Walsh MW (2011) The burden of pensions on states. New York Times. http://www.nytimes.com 10 March. Accessed 12 August 2011.

Chapter 3
The First Wave: Concession Bargaining in the 1980s

Abstract During the first wave of concession bargaining, occurring in the 1980s, employers were reacting to the pressures of global competition, domestic nonunion competition, and deregulation by insisting that unions lower labor costs. New collective agreements frequently had wage cuts or freezes, changes in work rules, and reduced pensions. Concession bargaining became widespread in the airlines (among the older, legacy carriers losing in their competitive battles with the low-cost carriers) and in domestic auto making, and then spread to other industrial sectors. The first wave of concession bargaining eroded the foundations of the labor accord (the accommodation underlying the relationship between unions and employers), freeing employers to incite the ultra-concession bargaining that would appear around the turn of the next century.

Keywords Concession bargaining • Ultra-concession bargaining • Airline negotiations • Airlines, the united autoworkers • The legacy airlines • The low-cost airlines • The Detroit Three automakers • The labor accord

It is difficult to say exactly when concession bargaining first became a prominent form of collective bargaining.[1] Collective agreements have been negotiated for nearly two centuries in the United States, and now and then employers demanded that unions roll back their past gains. In conventional collective bargaining, negotiators focus on stabilizing and furthering the union–management relationship (e.g., by developing a grievance procedure) while also agreeing to incremental adjustments in

[1] Some (e.g., Schiavone 2008; McCartin 2011) continue to argue that the breaking of the strike by air traffic controllers in 1981 (the PATCO strike) by President Reagan signaled to employers that antiunion extremism was entirely appropriate and effective, and that this example led directly to the concession bargaining of the 1980s. However, there is no evidence of any causal linkage between the defeat of the PATCO strikers and changes in employer bargaining strategies and tactics or the intensity of their antiunion campaigns during organizing drives.

G. Chaison, *The New Collective Bargaining*, SpringerBriefs in Economics,
DOI 10.1007/978-1-4614-4024-6_3,

the terms and conditions of employment (e.g., through multistage wage increases and cost-of-living adjustments to pay). Employment decisions (e.g., who should be hired, and how many workers should be hired?) are left to management. However, as we saw in the preceding chapter, concession bargaining is based on management taking control of the bargaining agenda and determining what will be bargained over. Management argues that the company's survival depends on rewriting the collective agreement and revamping how bargaining is done (Kochan and McKersie 1982; Townsend 1982).

Early Concession Bargaining

There were a few scattered cases of concession bargaining in the nineteenth century, but by the 1960s a distinct new employer approach to bargaining began to emerge.[2] Some employers demanded that unions reopen collective agreements and agree to pay cuts or less costly pensions and health care plans. Otherwise, plants would be closed and jobs lost. For example, in 1962 at Armour's meatpacking plant in Memphis, Tennessee, the Meat Cutters union agreed to reopen their contract for wage reductions, cancel a scheduled wage increase, and cut employee benefits—all so that management would not close the plant (Henle 1973). In the early 1970s, there was sporadic concession bargaining in the automobile, auto parts, electrical appliances, and food products industries. In each case, the employer threatened to fully or partially shut down operations due to either slackened consumer demand during a recession or because of its inability to defend against foreign competitors (Bell 1989). Unions heard at the bargaining table that there was an inevitable trade-off between wages and employment because management could transfers operations from higher-cost unionized plants to lower-cost nonunion ones.

A wave of concession bargaining began in the late 1970s and early 1980 as the full pressure of industry deregulation was felt at the airlines. During those years a surge in low-cost foreign competition created intense pressure for cost-cutting in basic manufacturing.[3] Negotiations in the 1980s were characterized as "concession prone" (Bell 1989, 44). One observer of the labor scene remarked: "Organized labor has recently given more ground on wage gains and restrictive work practices than at any time in the past 35 years" (Townsend 1982, 15). The rate of increase in wages in major collective agreements fell from 9.8 % in 1981 to 3.6 % in 1982. In 1982,

[2] For a bibliography of articles dealing with the early years of the first wave of concession bargaining, see Dworaczek (1984).

[3] For a review of the early years of the first wave of concessions see Henle (1973) and Mitchell (1982, 1983a, b). Case studies of the declining unionized manufacturing are found in Craypo and Nissen (1993).

43 % of workers covered under collective agreements had no wage increase for the first year of their collective agreements and 35 % had no increase over the term of their agreement (Kochan and McKersie 1983). One survey found that a quarter of the executives of large companies had negotiated concessions, and that "concessions have been granted by workers in hundreds of smaller companies." (Concessionary bargaining: Will the new cooperation last? 1982, 66)

During the first wave there were wide variations in concession bargaining outcomes. Some contracts imposed wage cuts and freezes. Others sought to raise production by redrafting work rules and expanding job classifications so workers would do more for the same pay (Kochan and McKersie 1983). The employer *modus operandi* quickly became apparent: they were using collective bargaining to cut labor costs knowing that union bargainers and union members would agree to cuts if jobs were clearly threatened. An observer of collective bargaining trends wrote "For organized labor, 1982 is shaping up as the *Year of the Giveback*. With major industries on the skids and jobs at risk, unions have already made some surprising concessions in this year's heavy round of bargaining, and more are expected" (Wilson 1982, 37).

The Airlines: The Cradle of Concession Bargaining

Concession bargaining became the norm at the airlines, an industry wracked by intense domestic competition in the wake of its 1978 deregulation (Cappelli and Harris 1985; Curtin 1986). When the airlines were deregulated (i.e., when they were free to choose their own routes and rates), they already had a long history of lengthy contract negotiations, bitter strikes after bargaining impasses, rejections of tentative agreements by union members, and splintered bargaining units (i.e., unions did not represent all the workers of an airline but rather specialized crafts such as pilots, flight attendants, mechanics, ramp workers, ticket agents, so that a single company might deal with a half-dozen unions) (Chaison 2006). In the throes of the intense competition between the older higher-cost airlines (the so-called legacy carriers—Alaska, American, Continental, Delta, Northwest, United, and US Airways) and the newer and smaller low-cost carriers (notably Southwest, AirTran, and JetBlue), the legacy carriers transformed conventional collective bargaining into concession bargaining (2007).[4]

[4] The legacy carriers were not able to compete with the low-cost carriers and the low-cost carriers kept their costs down by growing quickly. The low-cost carriers relied on point-to-point systems that did not integrate flights, instead focusing on low-cost traveling between sites. The legacy carriers used the hub and spoke system of operations under which passengers fly to hubs at major airports to connect to flights to their final destinations. This was a convenient way for traveling from small communities because it opened up worldwide routes, but it was 45 % more expensive than a point-to-point system (Chaison 2007).

Union–management relations at the airlines have always swung from one extreme to another. Sometimes they were highly collaborative as employers sought to build trust with unions as a prelude to moderate wage increases and greater productivity through relaxed work rules. But in times of intense competition, union–management relations were highly confrontational, as airlines threatened that there would either be concessions sufficient to offset rising operating costs or bankruptcy would be declared, collective agreements voided, and workers would be laid off.

In 1983, American Airlines negotiated a two-tier wage plan under which a fifth of its workforce was on the lower pay tier. Labor costs dropped by more than a third. But the plan had to be reversed in 1987 because of worker dissatisfaction and the company's inability to recruit a better workforce (Salpukas 1985). However, within 3 years of the American settlement, the two-tier structure was copied by most other airlines as a way to cut costs over time as workers left and new workers were hired (Bamber et al. 2009, 21).

In the decade after the 1978 deregulation, concession bargaining quickly spread among the legacy airlines. In bargaining with nearly all legacy carriers,' unions agreed to temporary wage cuts or freezes, two-tiered wage plans, and changes in work rules. In return, jobs were saved. By the 1990s, the tide of concession bargaining was greatly reduced, company profits were returning and bargaining power was shifting back to the unions (Dooley 1994). But the roots of concession bargaining remained at the heart of the industry's volatile labor relations and employer's demands for concessions would reappear when the hard times returned in a decade (Chaison 2007).

The Auto Industry: Setting the Trend

The automobile industry was the trendsetter for the first wave of concession bargaining because of its high-profile bargaining as a huge national industry and the long (nearly 50-year) relationship between the United Automobile Workers (UAW) and the Detroit Three (General Motors, Ford, and Chrysler).[5] Bargaining in autos was mature in the sense that there were clear understandings between union and management about what the results of conventional bargaining should be like in a broad sense, i.e., standard annual wage increases, an elaborate web of work rules that carefully defined and protected jobs, and a system of employee benefits that was the richest in manufacturing.[6] Collective bargaining fleshed out the details but

[5] For an argument that the concessions negotiated at the automakers in the early 1980s set the trend for unions granting concessions see Slaughter (1983).

[6] For an overview of the relationship between the UAW and GM from the earliest days of organizing in the 1930s to the bankruptcy of GM in 2009, see de Gier (2010).

the basis collective agreement pattern was set and time-honored. However, the UAW had been greatly weakened in the 1980s (it lost 23 % of its members from 1955 to 1985 (Gifford 2011))[7] as plants closed because carmakers shifted production overseas and imported cars captured a larger share of the domestic auto market. To add to the UAW's problems, foreign automakers opened plants in the United States (the so-called *transplants*) with intention of operating low-cost and nonunion.

The UAW had to agree to concessions to save jobs and the Detroit Three demanded nothing less than lower labor costs matched by higher productivity to restore and protect their competitive positions. For instance, in the early 1980s, Ford and the UAW agreed to wage concessions saving the company an estimated $1-billion over 30 months in return for a promise not to close any plants (Lanoutte 1982). In subsequent negotiations, the UAW gave up its traditional 3 % annual increase in base wages (Katz et al. 2002).

If the legacy airlines gave birth to industry-wide concession bargaining, it was at the Detroit Three that concession bargaining reached its full bloom. Seeing the widely publicized bargaining trends in the auto industry, other manufacturing companies quickly realized that aggressive bargaining could actually help them gain a competitive edge.

Concession Bargaining Spreads

Concession bargaining quickly spread through the unionized economy during the 1980s, following the examples of the airlines and the automakers. Employers in the maritime industry responded to growing competitive pressures by breaking away from national bargaining associations, bargaining on their own, and demanding that unions cut pensions and health care plans and changes to work rules to raise productivity (Donn 1989). In trucking, wages were frozen, the cost of living allowances were cut, and work rules were modified (Wilson 1982). In steel, a major bargaining settlement cut wage and holidays in 1983 (Mitchell 1983b). In meatpacking, wages were frozen and cost of living allowances were reduced. By 1982, a majority of government workers were covered by negotiated concessions (Bureau of National Affairs 1982). The construction industry, once widely known for its tough bargaining unions and high labor costs, accounted for 40 % of all wage cuts and freezes from 1981 to 1984 (Mitchell 1985).

In their study of concession bargaining among a wide variety of manufacturing companies in New England, Chaison and Plovnick (1986) observed a union–

[7] For a review of the state of the UAW following the decline of the domestic car producers, see Seetharam and Korkki (2011).

management reciprocity. As some employers argued for concessions, particularly those relaxing work rules, they had to open the door to greater union participation in decision-making on the shop floor level (e.g., work redesign and quality improvement) as well as the strategic level (e.g., decisions about automation in manufacturing and plant locations). Unions insisted on more than becoming junior partners in success and senior partners in failure. They argued that worker's sacrifices should lead to a sharing of profits and control, and that if unions were being asked to care more about company well-being they had to be fully informed about the company's present and future. Ironically, the first wave of concessions, imposed as it was by management, sometimes opened the door to experimentation with worker and union empowerment. The 1980s saw some shared power in multiple levels of committees dealing with everything from profit-sharing to production quality, plant relocation, and technological change (Concessionary bargaining: Will the new cooperation last? 1982; Mitchell 1985). It was unclear, however, whether experiments would take hold and whether real and lasting cooperation could actually grow from conflict. But more important, coinciding with sporadic information-sharing and labor–management cooperation, there was a dark side to first-wave concession bargaining. The very foundations of collective bargaining were being weaken.

The Labor Accord Begins to Fade Away

The first wave of concession bargaining severely strained the unions' and employer's shared understandings about the fundamentals of their relationship, commonly called the "labor accord," the "labor–management accord," or the "capital–labor accord" (Edwards and Podgursky 1986). Many labor relations researchers and practitioners believed that unions and employers had coexisted in the United States as nearly equals in the workplace and as partners in the employment relationship.[8] For instance, Chaison and Bigelow (2002, 21) concluded: "From the 1940s through the

[8] Some believed that the accord was neither entirely balanced nor pervasive. It was limited by geography (found mostly in heavily industrialized regions such as the Northeast) and by industry (primarily in manufacturing, mining, transportation, and construction). In these regions and industries, the workforce was so heavily unionized that employers had little to gain by resisting unions (Edwards and Podgursky 1986; Chaison and Bigelow 2002; Godard 2009). N. Lichtenstein, a major critic of the prevalence of the labor–management accord, wrote that the accord was "at best a brittle truce in which each side probed for weaknesses and division on the other side" (Lichtenstein 2011, 3). This critique is fully developed in Lichtenstein (2002, 98–140).

1970s, employers accommodated unions largely because of the high costs of avoiding them at nonunion facilities or dislodging them at nonunion ones.... Under the unions' and employers' tacit understanding about their mutual dealings ... unions accepted the right or employers to manage the enterprise within the bounds set by law and collective agreements, and employers accepted the right of unions to exist and negotiate collective agreements."[9] The essential assumption was that "management's job is to manage, and the union's is to object" (Strauss 1995, 342).

The accord began to unravel by the late 1970s as employers retreated from their commitment to collective bargaining, tried to repel unions during organizing drives, and suppressed unions at unionized firms.[10] By the 1980s, management was starting to demolish the accord; it had adopted an aggressive market-oriented strategy ideology that justified union opposition as a necessary struggle to preserve management flexibility in a highly competitive environment (Rogers 1993). Concession bargaining refuted the understandings inherent in conventional collective bargaining under the accord—the assumptions that the union acts and management reacts, that present settlements always added to past ones, and that bargaining may be adversarial but not malicious because it was a step in the ongoing union–management relationship (Chaison 2006). So when the first wave of concession bargaining receded in the 1990s, only the remnants of union–management accommodation were left in its wake.[11]

The first wave of concession bargaining had shown employers that it could be the preferred way to deal with unions. For a decade, the employers' insistence on concessions had become "bargaining as usual" (Bureau of National Affairs 1982; Miner 1982). Major settlements were being shaped almost entirely by market conditions, rather than the cost of living or other bargaining settlements in the industry or region. In negotiations, management's declarations about its inability to pay overwhelmed the unions (Wilson 1982). Concession bargaining receded by the end of the early or mid-1990s (Cutcher-Gershenfeld and Kochan 2004), but the mutual acceptance underlying the labor accord was severely strained.

[9] As Marshall (2011, 2) described the basic understanding between labor and management: "workers offered loyalty and labor offered peace to companies in return for stable jobs and decent pay and benefits."

[10] For a succinct discussion of the fundamental changes in American industrial relations in the early 1980s, see Mitchell (1983b, 83–90), Kochan (1986), and Nilsson (1997).

[11] As the accord unraveled so did workers' loyalty to their employers. Many workers had thought that they would be rewarded for their efforts with long-term employment but after their unions agreed to concessions, they found that their assumptions about long tenure were being ignored by their employer and they could easily lose their jobs (Korkki 2011).

References

Bamber G J et al. (2009) Up in the air: How airlines can improve performance by engaging their employees. Cornell University Press, Ithaca N.Y.

Bell L (1989) Union concessions in the 1980s. Fed. Res. Bank of New York Quarterly Rev. 14: 44–58.

Bureau of National Affairs (1982) Labor Relations in an economic recession: Job losses and concession bargaining. Bur. of Nat. Affairs, Washington D.C.

Cappelli P, Harris, TH (1985) Airline union concessions in the wake of deregulation. Mon. Labor Rev. 108: 37–38.

Chaison G (2006) Unions in America. Sage, Thousand Oaks, CA.

Chaison G (2007) Airline negotiations and the new concessionary bargaining. J. Lab. Res. 28: 643–657

Chaison G, Bigelow B (2002) Unions and legitimacy. Cornell University Press, Ithaca, NY.

Chaison G, Plovnick M (1986) Is there a new collective bargaining? California Manag. Rev. 28:54–61.

Concessionary bargaining: Will the new cooperation last? (1982) Bus. Week. 14 June: 66-69, 72, 77–81.

Craypo C, Nissen B (1993) Grand designs: The impact of corporate strategies on workers, unions, and communities. ILR Press, Ithaca N.Y.

Curtin WJ (1986) Airline deregulation and labor relations. Monthly Lab. Rev. 109: 29–31.

Cutcher-Gershenfeld J, Kochan T (2004) Taking Stock: Collective bargaining at the turn of the century. Ind. and Labor Relat. Rev. 58: 3–26.

De Gier E (2010) Paradise lost revisited: GM and the UAW in historical perspective. Visiting fellow working papers. Paper 30 www.digitalcommons.ilr.cornell/edu. 1 September. Accessed 10 February 2012.

Dooley FJ (1994) Déjà vu for airline labor relations. J Labor Res. 15: 169–190.

Donn CB (1989) Concession bargaining in the ocean going maritime industry. Ind. Labor Rel. Rev. 42: 189–200.

Dworaczek M (1984) Labor concessions in collective bargaining: An article bibliography. Vance Bibliographies: Monticello, Ill.

Edwards R., Podgursky M (1986) The unraveling accord: American unions in crisis. In Edwards R et al. (eds) Unions in crisis and beyond: perspectives from six countries. Auburn, Dover MA.

Gifford C (2011) Directory of U.S. labor organizations. Bur. of Nat. Aff., Washington D.C.

Godard J (2009) The exceptional decline of the American labor movement. Ind. Labor Rel. Rev. 63: 82–108.

Henle P (1973) Reverse collective Bargaining: A look at some union concession situations. Indus. and Lab. Rel. Rev. 26:956–968.

Katz et al. (2002) Autos: Continuity and change in collective bargaining. In Clark PF, Delaney JT and Frost A (eds) Collective bargaining in the private sector. IRRA, Madison, WI: 55–90.

Kochan, TA (1986) The future of collective bargaining and its implications for labor arbitration. Sloan School of Management, Working paper 1787–86, MIT, Cambridge MA.

Kochan TA, McKersie RB(1982) Interpreting current developments in collective bargaining and industrial relations, Unpublished paper, Sloan School of Management, MIT: Cambridge MA.

Kochan T A, McKersie RB (1983) SMR Forum: Collective bargaining—pressures for change. Sloan Management Rev. 23: 59–65.

Korkki P (2011) The search: The shifting definition of worker loyalty. New York Times. 24 April: 8.

Lanoutte W J (1982) Recession brings labor-management closer on union contracts. National J. 6 March: 422–425.

Lichtenstein N (2002) State of the union. Princeton N.J., Princeton University Press.

Lichtenstein N (2011) The long history of labor bashing. The Chronicle of Higher Education, The Chronical Review, www.chronicle.com 6 March. Accessed 15 February 2012.

Marshall W (2011) Why labor needs a new deal for labor and business. The Atlantic www.theatlantic.com 4 September. Accessed 6 September 2011.
McCartin J (2011) The strike that busted unions. New York Times. www.nytimes.com 2 August. Accessed 2 August 2011.
Miner T (1982) Concession bargaining. Chicago-Kent Law Rev. 59: 981–996.
Mitchell DJB (1982) Recent union contract concessions. Brookings Papers on Econ. Activity 1: 165–201.
Mitchell DJB (1983a) Is wage determination at a turning point? Proceedings of the 35th Annual Meeting of the Indust. Rel. Res. Assoc.: 354–361.
Mitchell DJB (1983b) The 1982 union wage concessions: A turning point for collective bargaining. California Manag. Rev. 25: 78–92.
Mitchell DJB (1985) Concession bargaining and wage determination. Bus. Econ. 7: 45–50.
Nilsson EA (1997) The growth of union decertification: A test of two non-nested theories. Ind. Relat. 36: 324–348.
Rogers J (1993) Don't worry, be happy: The postwar decline of private-sector unionism in the United States, in Jenson J, Mahon R. (1993) (eds) The challenge of restructuring. Temple University Press, Philadelphia: 48–71.
Salpukas A (1985) The two-tier wage impact. New York Times October 30:1.
Schiavone M (2008) Unions in crisis?: The future of organized labor in America. Praeger, Westport CT.
Slaughter J (1983) Concession bargaining in autos. Labor Res. Rev. 1:70–72.
Strauss G (1995) Is the new deal system collapsing: With what might it be replaced? Indust. Rel. 33: 329–349.
Townsend E. (1982) Unions grow reluctant to make concessions to troubled industries. Christian Science Monit. June 24:15.
Wilson M (1982) Big labor faces reality. Dun's Bus. Mon. February: 37–42.

Chapter 4
The Second Wave of Concession Bargaining: The New Ultra-Concession Bargaining

Abstract Concession bargaining reappeared with great intensity and frequency at the start of the twenty-first century. We witnessed a new *ultra-concession bargaining* that was not based on the usual assumptions of the 1980s first-wave concession bargaining. Ultra-concession bargaining began at the airlines, was widely adapted, again, by the Detroit Three (the Detroit automakers, i.e., General Motors, Ford, and Chrysler) and the auto parts makers, and then spread through manufacturing. It took hold in the public sector as employers tried not only to cut labor costs to reduce budget gaps but also to weaken and displace unions as well. Six brief bargaining profiles and a review of the union upheaval in Wisconsin suggest the diversity and intensity of the new collective bargaining.

Keywords Ultra-concession bargaining • The Detroit Three • Auto negotiations • Auto parts makers negotiations • UAW • Wage freezes • Wage cuts • Voluntary employee beneficiary association • The California grocery strike • Two-tier wage systems • Public sector bargaining • Wisconsin

In the years since the start of the twenty-first century, concession bargaining reappeared with great intensity. The tables were again turned on unions and employers. The labor accord—the labor–management accommodation that was described in the preceding chapter—was quickly eroding. And now employers presented their demands in a way that was more threatening than pleading; their patience with the "burden" of unions and collective bargaining had worn thin. The usual *quid pro quo* that was the heart of concession bargaining was missing or unclear in negotiations—unions now expected little or nothing in return for making concessions. Jobs might be saved, but then they might also be lost. A plant might remain open or a new work-shift added in return for concessions but the plant might soon be shuttered or

G. Chaison, *The New Collective Bargaining*, SpringerBriefs in Economics,
DOI 10.1007/978-1-4614-4024-6_4,

the work-shift ended. Nothing could be guaranteed. Gone was the usual assumption that concession bargaining would not have to be repeated. This year's concessions never precluded the next year's. And employers justified their demands for concessions simply by saying that they wanted them.

Employers again used collective bargaining to lower operating costs. Union officers might reminisce about their past understandings with employers, but there was little they could do to stop the management offensive. At the most, union officers might direct their energies and wiles to retaining past gains, but forward progress was usually out of the question.

Once again, concession bargaining emerged from the hypercompetitive world of the airlines and reached full bloom in autos. It then spread to the auto parts makers and to a wide variety of industries ranging from groceries to light manufacturing, and—in a second wave of the second wave—it enveloped the public sector.

Again, the Airlines

So much was happening in the airlines that it seemed to be an industry set on fast-forward. Chaison (2007, 2) remarked:

> ...in just the second half of 2005, two major carriers (Delta Airlines and Northwest Airlines) declared bankruptcy; there was a bitter strike of mechanics and cleaners at Northwest; the pilots at Delta Airlines agreed to a 14 % pay cut and those at Northwest agreed to a 24 % cut; the cost of jet fuel (a major operating expense) increased by nearly 50 %; United Airlines was successful putting together a business plan and financial backing that would soon get it out a 3-year bankruptcy; and industry conditions appeared to be changing from sharply declining to moderately improving.[1]

In the 1980s, the heads of the older or *legacy* airlines (i.e., those operating before industry deregulation in 1978) worried about how to adjust to new competition from the younger low-cost carriers in a deregulated environment. Now they

[1] Chaison (2007, 2) also wrote "For intensity and complexity, there is nothing quite like airline labor relations." The airlines became known for its hard bargaining because, as mentioned in the preceding chapter, competition between companies was intense, the industry was heavily unionized, and negotiations were fragmented. Some employers dealt with as many as five different unions, each representing a different craft (e.g., pilots, flight attendants, ramp workers, ticket agents, and mechanics), though some operated nonunion (e.g., JetBlue), and employers frequently negotiate with unions while declaring bankruptcy. In addition, labor relations was volatile because of unpredictable external shocks, such as swings in the price of jet fuel and fluctuating consumer preferences.

had to deal not only with competition from low-cost carriers, but with higher operating costs due to the spike in a fuel prices[2] and with lower consumer demand because so many regular passengers were reluctant to fly due to the possibility of terrorism after the 9/11 attacks. A return to concession bargaining seemed the fastest, most direct way to lower operating costs. The concessions that were demanded and agreed to were usually massive, set high to offset huge operating losses. For example, in 2004 the pilots at Delta Airlines ratified a 5-year collective agreement with a wage cut of 32.5 % (or a reduction in the salary of the highest paid pilots of about $90,000 per year). The contracts created $1 billion per year in company savings—not nearly enough because Delta had lost nearly $10 billion since 2000 (Maynard 2004a). One expert commented that airline bargaining lacked the give-and-take that was usual in conventional negotiations and even many of the 1980s concession bargaining contexts. "I've never seen bargaining like this before. The company is just talking a lead and the unions are reacting" (Maynard 2004b, C4). And now the carriers were using bankruptcy to magnify their bargaining power (Chaison 2007).

Under the law of bankruptcy, a company's financial obligations are suspended pending the resolution of its reorganization or liquidation. It is possible for a company to nullify and rewrite its collective bargaining agreements in bankruptcy court, but this is not easy. The company's trustees must first submit proposed contract changes to the union, meet in good faith with the union to negotiate changes, have the proposal rejected without good cause (in the view of the bankruptcy court), and then receive permission from the court to make the necessary changes (Becker 1981; Feldacker 2000; Pettit 2008; Gerdano 2012).[3] While it is certainly not easy to revoke collective agreements in bankruptcy court, a company's threat to try it, or to at least freeze the pension plan as a prelude to bankruptcy, is usually enough to get unions to agree to demands for concessions.

[2] It has been estimated that it takes a 1 % increase in revenues to cover a 4–5 % increase in fuel costs. The cost of aviation fuel has gone up tremendously over the past decade and this lead to greatly increased fares to offset rising operating costs. For instance, in 2001 airlines spent $14.8 billion on fuel and their fuel bill was $38.4 in 2006 (Michels 2008). From 2002 to 2005, wages and benefits of airline workers were cut by an estimated $11 billion, primary through concession bargaining, despite rising company profits (Finamore 2007). Labor shares of total operating expenses fell from 37 % in 2002 to 25 % in 2006 largely because of negotiated wage and benefit cuts and the rising price of fuel (Hirsch 2007).

[3] The Bankruptcy Code does, however, permit interim changes in collective bargaining agreements when these are seemed essential to the continuation of the business and necessary to prevent irreparable harm (Feldacker 2000; Gerdano 2012).

Bankruptcy became commonplace to airline bargaining[4] (Greenhouse 2003a; Maynard 2003a, 2004c; Bailey 2006; Vail 2012). United Airlines, for example, became masterful at coordinating bankruptcy and collective bargaining. United was in Chapter 11 bankruptcy[5] for 38 months (December 9, 2002 to February 1, 2006)—the longest ever for an airline. Soon after declaring bankruptcy it pressured its unions to renegotiate collective agreements, threatening to have the agreements rescinded if a settlement could not be reached. It negotiated concessions valued at $2.56 billion annually for 6 years. In August 2004, United terminated its employees' pension plans with court permission, replacing them with less beneficial ones. A year later, while threatening to petition a bankruptcy judge to reject the existing collective agreements, United negotiated a second round of wage and benefit cuts for an additional $700 million in savings. (Among these concessions were a 5-year agreement with the flight attendants that cut wages by 9.5 %.) During its years of bankruptcy, United was able to cut $7 billion in annual operating costs and lay off a quarter of its workforce (Chaison 2006).

The Detroit Automakers

Bargaining in autos was between the UAW, a union that understood the financial troubles of the industry, and the Detroit Three (GM, Ford, and Chrysler), troubled companies that knew that the union saw its mission as, first and foremost, protecting job security and pay and benefits of the members. The two had been bargaining for 7 decades. Negotiations followed a predictable pattern—the UAW negotiated against a target company and threatened to impose the settlement on the other two with the threat of a strike—and a standard agreement (that included a usual wage increase of 3 %, protections against inflation and job loss (e.g., workers who were

[4] From 1978 (the year of industry deregulation) through 2005, 167 airlines filed for bankruptcy: 152 were for Chapter 11 bankruptcies (i.e., reorganizations as opposed to court supervised liquidations through Chapter 7). From 2001 to 2005, there were 21 airline bankruptcies. Three bankruptcies (United, Northwest, and Delta) were among the largest corporate bankruptcies ever, with combined assets of nearly 60 billion dollars (Chaison 2007). In November 2011, the parent company of American Airlines filed for bankruptcy. The airlines said that a key reason for declaring bankruptcy was the urgent need to reduce labor costs and reach competitive levels. Two weeks prior to the bankruptcy the pilots had rejected proposals for 7 and 9 % wage increases in return for longer working hours and few contributions to their pension plans (De La Merced 2011; Nicas and Spector 2011; Lahart 2012). There were rumors in early 2012 that there were several potential buyers for American Airlines including Delta Airlines and a private equity firm with a history of airline investments. A buyout might be contingent upon lower labor costs through concession bargaining (Chon et al. 2012). In early February 2012, American Airlines announced its intent to cut labor costs by 20 % and eliminate 15,000 jobs or more. The company wanted to slash spending by $2 billion per year and raise revenues annually by $1 billion as part of its plan in bankruptcy court to return to profitability. Wages and pensions would be cut through concession bargaining with the company's three unions (Carey and Nicas 2012; Koenig 2012).

[5] Bankruptcy for reorganization rather than for liquidation (Chapter 7).

laid off would be referred to a "jobs bank" for future placement and would continue to receive most of their pay and benefits just for being willing to transfer)).

But in the first decade of this century, the Detroit Three were barely surviving. They were making too many large cars and light trucks for a market that had changed substantially (consumers wanted smaller, more fuel-efficient vehicles). Their production capacity was oversized for the shrinking auto market in North America. In 2000, US auto sales were at 17.8 million; 8 years later the figure was at 13.5 million and falling (Chrysler 2009). Potential auto buyers were finding prices too high and credit too scarce.

The Detroit automakers seemed to have discovered the formula for failure—they produced cars at less than full capacity and sold cars at less than full price. Foreign auto companies, especially those with plants in the United States (the so-called *transplants*) were winning a larger and larger share of the market and operating at lower costs because of their newer and more efficient production facilities and younger nonunion workforces.[6] The Detroit Three felt as if they were about to collapse under the weight of their huge production facilities and the lavish benefits provided to both employed and retired autoworkers (Maynard 2003b; Dziczek et al. 2008; Krisher 2008; Vlasic and Bunkley 2008; Stoll 2009; Shapiro 2011). A Wall Street Journal editorial said what many must have been thinking but few dared say; "There is no natural law that America must have a Detroit automotive industry any more than steel has to be made for all time in Bethlehem, Pennsylvania or textiles in New England" (America's other auto industry 2008, A22).

Plants and dealerships would have to be closed, product lines (e.g., Pontiac, Saturn Oldmobile at GM) cut, and thousands of jobs eliminated for the Detroit Three to survive. The auto crisis may have been caused more by shrinking consumer demand than by intolerable costs, but restructuring—operating leaner and cheaper—seemed the most popular cure for the industry's woes. There was a widespread belief, created by the federal government and its Auto Task Force, that the Detroit Three were not only too big to fail but too big to survive—they could only prosper as smaller companies with fewer plants, car models, workers, and dealers, and they had to somehow thrive or the local (particularly Detroit), state (particularly Michigan), and indeed the national economy would be in shambles (Chaison 2006). Two of the three companies (General Motors and Chrysler) went into bankruptcies, guided by the federal government, that were designed to protect collective bargaining agreements (Cho and Mufson 2008). Prior to bankruptcy, autoworkers were being offered, and were accepting in large numbers, buyouts to leave their jobs. The jobs bank program was eliminated. Federal loans were given to the Detroit Three, but under the condition that they cut their operating costs and narrow the gap between their labor costs and those of their transplant competitors (Cho and Goldfarb 2008). The stage was set for wage freezes or cuts, two-tier wage systems, and reductions in pensions and health care benefits.

---

[6] For a description of the UAW's unsuccessful attempts to unionize workers at foreign-owned US auto plants, see Dolan (2011b).

One controversial concession, the VEBA (Voluntary Employee Beneficiary Association) plans, was negotiated by the UAW and the Detroit Three. They transferred the obligations to provide health care benefits for retirees from the companies to trustee committees. (The structure and objective of VEBAs were mentioned in the second chapter). The automakers' VEBAs attracted huge public attention because of the misconception that, because VEBAs were partly paid for by company stock, the UAW somehow now owned the automakers. Actually, just the opposite was true. The VEBAs had trustee committee with union representatives who were not acting independently but serving as interests of retirees. The UAW always saw the VEBAs as bargaining concessions and were concerned that if they were underfunded and they would not offset rising costs of health care for retirees. Moreover, VEBAs could compromise the union, putting the UAW in the position of cutting back on the health care benefits of its retired members to keep VEBAs afloat. As one union officer stated: "The union is not a financial institution. The union's purpose is to advance social justice and not manage the retreat from corporate accountability" (Kutalik 2007, 1).

The Detroit Three's VEBAs were gigantic. For example, in 2007 GM's UAW members approved a VEBA for $46.7 billion to cover $64.3 billion (73 %) of the costs of retirees' health care plans. Of this amount, GM contributed cash, funds from an existing health care trust, and financial notes convertible into company stock.[7] The VEBA did enable GM to take a large liability off its books and appear to be a stronger company to lenders (Chaison 2006).

By 2010, just 3 years after its last major concessions were negotiated, the auto industry was turning around. All signs pointed to revival. The Detroit automakers, under pressure from the government and competitors, were finally producing the smaller, economical cars that were more attractive to consumers. Auto sales in the United States rebounded in 2010 and, although not reaching earlier highs, the Detroit Three were clearly regaining the favor of consumers and building a foundation for future growth (Bunkley 2011a, c; Durbin and Krisher 2011). In the first quarter of 2011 the automakers had a combined profit of $6 billion (Detroit, the union and improving times 2011), jobs were being added rather than cut, and the breakeven points at which producers became profitable were lowered (Bunkley 2011b; Headapohl 2011; Vlasic 2011a; Terlep 2012). In 2011, General Motors earned a record, $9.19 billion in net income (Higgins 2012) enabling each worker to receive a $7,000 profit-sharing check (Roberson 2012). In 2011, Ford had a net income of over 20 billion dollars and the hard times seemed well behind (Hirsch 2012).[8]

---

[7] In exchange for the VEBA and other concessions, GM promised new products for 16 US assembly plants and said it would hire 3,000 temporary workers at full wages and benefits.

[8] For the arguments that the auto profits of 2011 do not signal a sustained recovery see, for example, Jakab (2012). He believes that sales were being pushed up by pent-up consumer demand because so few cars were bought in 2008–2010, that recent warm weather may have increased sales, and that the full reentry of Japanese producers into the market would eventually depress domestic sales.

Most important, the gap between the hourly wage of unionized autoworkers and nonunion ones at the transplants was narrowing (Naughton and Lippert 2011; Detroit, the union and improving times 2011).

An auto industry turnaround can also lead to some unique bargaining problems for the Detroit Three by creating expectations for the reduction or end of past concessions (Bunkley 2011c; Shapiro 2011; Vlasic 2011a, c). In September 2011, the UAW started negotiations with the Detroit Three. General Motors was the target company, and bargained with first, forming the pattern for negotiations with Ford and Chrysler. The new agreements, ratified by the union members, had signing bonuses, lump-sum payments, new profit-sharing arrangements, wage increases for lower-tier workers, and employer promises to create jobs through reopening or expanding plants and production shifts to plants that were slated to be idle. But past concessions were only partially reversed, causing the head of a UAW local to comment: "…it's not a great contract, but it's a decent contract in tough times… In this contract, you didn't get a lot of gains, but you didn't lose anything either" (Snavely 2011, 1).

The 2011 settlements were fairly inexpensive, raising annual labor costs by only about 1 % (Vlasic 2011b). The UAW and its members understood that concessions made during the past decade could not be completely reversed in a single round of bargaining, and jobs would be saved and created only if operating costs could be contained, i.e., workers would have to be rewarded with bonus-type payments and profit-sharing payments without saddling the companies with fixed labor costs that could hurt them in their competition with the Japanese and Korean rivals. Concession bargaining had become the "new normal" in the auto industry (Woodall 2011). The lesson learned was that concessions were easy to get into but hard to get out of.

The Auto Parts Makers

Concession bargaining became entrenched in auto parts manufacturing with the agreement negotiated in 2006 between Delphi Corp, the nation's largest auto parts maker, and the UAW. Delphi was spun off from General Motors in May 1999, and GM became the company's largest customer. At the time of the split, GM agreed to be responsible for providing health care and pension benefits for Delphi retirees if Delphi filed for bankruptcy in 8 years (by 2007). So bargaining became three way, with the UAW negotiating against Delphi and GM. In March 2006, Delphi, GM, and the United Auto Workers reached agreement on an employee buyout scheme that would reduce employment at GM by 131,000 workers and Delphi by 13,000. Despite such severe cost-cutting, Delphi went into bankruptcy and petitioned the court to rescind its collective bargaining agreements. Believing it had a strong hand against the UAW and that not reaching a collective agreement would bring down GM and along with it the entire domestic auto industry, Delphi made some radical demands. First, in bargaining in October 2005, it demanded that hourly wages be cut to $9.00 from an average of $27.00. A few months later it raised its demand to $12.50 per hour and then went up to $22.00 per hour in July 2006 (to be reduced to $16.50 per hour for workers accepting a $50,000 lump-sum payment or "buy-down" for accepting the lower wage cut). The company also demanded a lower wage tier for new hires, set at $10.00 per hour. If its wage demands were not accepted, Delphi threatened to take the drastic steps of laying off 24,000 of its 34,000 production workers, closing 21 of its 29 plants, freezing payments to its pension plans, outsourcing all nonproduction work (e.g., building maintenance and truck repair) to outside companies, and eliminating the health care benefits of retirees (Chaison 2007). In June 2007, Delphi finally reached an agreement with the UAW that the unions' members would ratify and GM offered job buyouts to 24,000 Delphi workers.[9] Hourly wages were cut from $27 per hour to $14.50–$18.00 per hour (Bunkley 2007).

The workers at Delphi felt tremendous pressure to accept lower wages. "Many of those who supported the wage-cutting agreement say they had little choice but to do so. Without a ratified deal, Delphi had asked…[the judge of the bankruptcy court] to impose deeper cuts on workers" (Bunkley 2007, 1). If Delphi could not lower operating costs and restructure it might not survive bankruptcy, and it would drag down General Motors and intensify the severity of the economic recession. Using the possible crisis as leverage, Delphi was able to negotiate major cost-cutting concessions.

Visteon is the other major parts producer. In 1999, Ford spun off Visteon with initial coverage under the Ford collective agreement and a guarantee of terms of employment similar to those of Ford workers for 8 years (Katz et al. 2002). But Visteon did poorly and went into bankruptcy in 2009. As a condition of exiting bankruptcy, the unionized Visteon workers accepted a lump-sum wage payment, a two-tiered wage system, and a health care plan with reduced benefits.

And so, by the end of 2008, two-tiered wage systems were in the collective agreements of not only the Detroit Three automakers but also the two major auto parts makers. Concession bargaining was now deeply entrenched in the auto industry.

Concessions Spread

Since the start of the twenty-first century, a wide variety of employers demanded concessions, but it was the negotiations with major grocery chains in California that became the archetype of the new bargaining. In 2004, grocery workers at three major California chains—Kroger, Safeway, and Albertson—went on a long (141 days) and costly ($1.5–$2.5 billion in revenues lost) strike. The eventual settlement, ratified by 86 % of the strikers, included two-tiered systems for both wages and health care benefits (Chaison 2007; Weir 2007). The employers lost market share

[9] Delphi workers received $140,000 for those with 10–26 years of seniority or $70,000 for those with 1–10 years (Maynard and Bunkley 2006).

during the strike, and the strikers went into heavy personal debt (Huffstutter 2011). In the next round of negotiations, neither side wanted another costly strike,[10] and the union was able to win back most of its concessions; the companies had been disappointed with the two-tiered systems because they had not generated the expected savings and seriously divided the workforce (Cooper 2007). The 2004 strike was caused largely by the three company's fear of having to compete against the low-cost Wal-Mart "super-stores" that had been planned for Southern California. However, it was the size of the strike (at 60,000 workers, one of the largest strikes in decades), the backgrounds of the strikers (mostly unskilled workers who previously had little say about their terms of employment), and the cost-cutting settlement that made the California grocery strike the "poster child" of tough bargaining (Chaison). Three huge employers, fearful of new low-cost competition, were using collective bargaining to cut costs. To the companies, bargaining was something to control for gain, rather than a process to simply get through.

Throughout unionized America, companies were giving concession bargaining a try. For example, in 2003 Tyson Foods presented its workers union with a radical collective bargaining proposal—a 4-year wage freeze, the elimination of a profit-sharing plan, a two-tier wage system, more expensive health care benefits, and cuts in vacation time, sick leave, and pension benefits. The union went on strike for nearly a year, but ended up settling on the employer's terms, fearing that the striker replacements hired by the company might soon vote to have the union decertified as bargaining agent.[11] In 2008, Hollywood writers had agreed to significantly lower pay and benefits, as did actors in their negotiations, raising concerns that subsequent negotiations would be particularly contentious as the unions and their members try to get everything back at once (Cieply 2011). In 2011, a group of developers and real estate executives in New York, New Jersey, and Connecticut asked for major concessions from construction unions. Arguing that builders could no longer survive with high labor costs, the civic group asked for changes in work rules and benefits that would bring the union–nonunion differential closer to 10 % from the present 20–30 % (Bagli 2011).[12] Also in 2011, Verizon insisted on higher worker contributions to health care plans and reduced pension payoff (Troianovski 2011). Verizon's unions went on strike because they believed that the company's demand for wage and benefit cuts would "push workers out of the middle class" (Greenhouse 2011d).

---

[10] The employers could not afford the lost profit and market share, and the union feared that they would have little public sympathy if the workers voluntarily walked off their jobs in the midst of the recession (No S. Calif. grocery strike 2011).

[11] Tyson Workers reject… (2004). One reporter placed the Tyson negotiations and strike in context: …"Tyson has joined hundreds of companies nationwide demanding concessions from organized labor. As corporations grapple with a weak economy, fierce overseas competition, and soaring health care costs, they have made concessions a focus of labor negotiations…" Greenhouse (2003b, 12).

[12] In addition to the recommendation that some costly work rules be eliminated, the report lists at the conclusion of its Framework for Cost Reduction, "A 20 % reduction in the wage/benefit package" (Vitullo-Martin and Cohen 2011, 52).

Uchitelle (2010, A1) saw an ominous new change in how bargaining was done; "Demands for wages and benefit cuts were once mostly limited to money-losing companies like airlines or steel mills, whose survival seemed at stake. But now profitable companies were demanding concessions in the name of remaining competitive." Concession bargaining could now occur anywhere.

The Public Sector: The Second Wave of the Second Wave

We usually think of government workers as immune to the labor cost problems of the private sector because their employers seem to face little direct competition and unlimited treasury freezes. But the layoffs and wage and benefit cuts of private employees sooner or later reduce tax revenues, forcing cities and states to close budget gaps and to look for ways to reduce services or contract out government services to private providers (Powell 2011).

Public employers claimed that concessions must be granted by unions in bargaining or there would be mass layoffs.[13] In particular, they pointed out public workers usually pay a lower share of their health care plans than do private sector workers and that it is only fair that they agree to larger co-payments or deductibles (McKersie 2011). All that unions could do was to deflect the pressure for lower benefits and wages and to argue that cost savings should be found elsewhere, for example, by eliminating wasteful contracts with vendors (e.g., Dolan 2011a).

In the view of many, the pensions of public employees (mostly plans of the defined-benefit type) became unsustainable to the degree that there is now "pension envy"—the feeling among private sector workers whose pensions were frozen or reduced that public workers' pension should not receive special protections (Cooper and Walsh 2011; Greenhouse 2011c, e; Suroweicki 2011). State administrators and legislators began to consider bankruptcy and the rewriting of collective bargaining agreements if unions did not agree to pension cuts or freezes (Walsh 2011a, b).[14]

With their huge budgetary shortfalls,[15] many states sought to strip public employees bargaining rights as a prelude to concession bargaining. They limited the subjects of bargaining (for instance, by excluding health care benefits) and they

[13] For example, the city of Detroit was threatened with the possibility of being administered by an emergency manager who would cut operating costs if the Mayor and city council could not get the public employee unions to agree to concessions in bargaining (Dolan 2012).

[14] In 2011, it was estimated that nationwide, state, and local pension funds faced a shortfall of $3 trillion. In many states, more money was being paid to retirees than collected from state employees' pay and workers' taxes combined. As funds shrank, public employers faced the difficult choice of either cutting back on services or paying less in pensions than had been promised to retirees (and face possible law suits) (Walsh 2011b).

[15] In 2011 46 states had budget shortfalls totaling about 20 % of what they had planned to spend (Bluestone 2011).

weakened unions as organizations (for instance, by taking away their *check-off*, the automatic deduction of dues from members' paychecks or requiring that they reapply annually for certification). The traditional public sector bargaining outcomes suddenly became unbearably expensive (e.g., Masters et al. 2010; Mitchell 2010; Public-worker unions confront U.S. governors over benefits in role switch 2011; Wisniewski 2010). As Smith and Haberman (2011, 1) described the developing pressure: "Spurred by state budget crunches and an angry public mood, Republican and some Democratic leaders are focusing with increasing intensity on public workers and the unions that represent them, casting them as overpaid obstacles to good government and demanding cuts in their often-generous benefits."

Feeling that the voters were on their side, elected officials became emboldened, demanding that groups of public employees such as teachers and clerical workers accept wage freezes or job cuts and give up job security (e.g., Chupaska 2011; Kittilstad 2011; Mewes 2011; Powell 2011). Once so powerful and militant, the public sector unions now found that they had fallen into disfavor with public administrators and elected officials and had to deal with the ultra-concession bargaining that become acceptable to voters in the name of cost-cutting (Schoen 2011; Walsh 2011a, b). A report on public budgets and bargaining concluded: "…the shape of municipal budgets has been heavily influenced by *hard* bargaining between labor and management (emphasis added)." There was a "tense labor-management dialogue, in which unions are being forced to choose among painful alternatives"—employee benefits or employment (Pew Charitable Trusts 2009, 1). In this aggressive, often vindictive concession bargaining—which I call the "second wave of the second wave of concession bargaining"—governors, mayors, and county executives threatened massive layoffs and then told unions that this could be averted, at least for a while, if there were cost-cutting concessions.[16]

Hard bargaining became bargaining as usual throughout the public sector. For example, in San Bernadino County in Southern California, firefighters agreed to have their pensions and their pay cut to avoid layoffs (San Bernadino 2011). In Sterling Heights, outside of Detroit, the firefighters approved an agreement that cut pay by 10% when the employer assured them that cuts would insulate them from layoffs. It was the sixth bargaining group in the city that had agreed to concessions in bargaining to save jobs, and in the previous year the firefighters had accepted an agreement with a wage freeze and pension reductions (Delany 2011). In the Dallas School District, the teachers' union agreed to a 5-year contract that included 3 years of wage freezes, and a greater share of the cost of tuition for teacher training courses to be paid for by teachers (Moody 2011). In Worcester, Massachusetts, teachers' jobs that were slated for cuts were restored after the municipal employers and unions agreed to reductions in health care benefits (Foskett 2011). In Connecticut and New York State, mass layoffs were threatened when state employee unions rejected

[16] For reviews of municipal concession bargaining over the past decade, see Pew Charitable Trusts (2009).

wage freeze and cuts (Applebone 2011; Kaplan 2011). In New Jersey, employee benefits were rolled back in bargaining with all large groups of public workers (Perez-Pena 2011; Powell 2011). In Ohio, unions of teachers agreed to concessions (mostly wage freezes) valued at $700 million for the 2010 school year (Brownfield 2011). In San Diego County, employee pensions were cut in ten cities, often by reducing pension of newly hired workers after concession bargaining (Gustafson 2012).

Public sector unions may have once thought they could pass unscathed through economic hardship, but in the first decade of the century they faced stiff employer opposition in collective bargaining, often for the first time. Politicians, who once thought it wise to befriend public sector unions and win their campaign endorsements and campaign help, now found that it made more sense politically to fight unions. Riling the unions in the name of protecting the public treasury became the right thing to do politically.[17]

A Half Dozen Profiles of the New Ultra-Concession Bargaining, Plus One Upheaval

In a half dozen selected cases, we see brief portraits of the scope and diversity of the new ultra-concession bargaining. Each case shows a remarkable lack of employer restraint—management is not the least reluctant to threaten unions and union members. Unions faced a tough choice—either they agree to cut labor costs or jobs will be lost. This happens without any guarantees that further concession bargaining would be avoided or that further cuts would not be needed. And there was no sense of finality. Concessions could be demanded again—maybe next year, maybe in the next round of bargaining. Moreover, the new concession bargaining included a vast range of situations, from professional musicians working at a top-ranked symphony orchestra to workers picking apples for apple juice. One employer was an airline, another made airplanes; one employer was a famous maker of motorcycles in Wisconsin, and another was a famous maker of marine motors in the same state. Finally, one employer, also in Wisconsin, was at the vanguard of a national movement to weaken the unions, starting in the public sector where they were once most powerful.

[17] In 2012, towns and cities with budget deficits seriously considered declaring bankruptcy and following the path of automakers, auto parts makers, and airlines by pressing unions for wage cuts and freezes under the threat of abrogating collective agreements in bankruptcy court. In February 2012, the city of Stockton, California had a budget deficit of $20–40 million and was on the verge of declaring bankruptcy because there was little chance of closing the budget gap with citizens of mostly modest incomes and a 19 % unemployment rate in the surrounding area. With its population of 291,000, Stockton was large enough to draw national attention to the public sector bankruptcy concession bargaining option.

Northwest Airlines: As Bad As It Gets

Arguably the most bitter negotiation and strike since the start of this century was between Northwest Airlines and its union of mechanics and cleaners—the Aircraft Mechanics Fraternal Association (AMFA)—in 2005. This was ultra-concession bargaining at its most mean-spirited.

Northwest had proposed a 26 % wage and benefit cut in negotiations and AMFA responded with an offer to accept a 16 % cut, which would save the company $100 million annually.[18] Northwest's cost-cutting target was $1.1 billion from all its unions and it estimated that AMFA's share of the sacrifice should be $203 million (Northwest Airlines 2005). The head of Northwest stated that the alternative to its proposed cut would be a reduction in the workforce by half and a cut in the wages of the remaining workers by at least 25 %.

At an impasse in bargaining, AMFA called its 4,400 members out on strike. AMFA's picket lines were not honored by the unionized pilots and flight attendants; AMFA was considered to be a renegade union, a pariah in the labor movement because it had organized new members by winning groups of workers already represented by other unions (notably the Machinists) and criticizing unions that agreed to concessions in earlier airline bargaining (Marks 2005).[19] The AMFA strike became extremely bitter as the company replaced the striking mechanics, no unions came to the aide of AMFA, and AMFA claimed that Northwest's flights were unsafe. But the public continued to fly Northwest and the MFA members walked their picket lines to no effect.

AMFA even accused Northwest of provoking a strike so that it would have an excuse for filing for bankruptcy and trying to gut the collective agreement. The Northwest-AMFA strike was the largest in 2005 in days idle (371,700 days of idleness) and the second largest in length (91 days). The company was prepared for the strike and brought in replacement mechanics from the start, hoping that it could continue operations and not lose customers.

Northwest threatened to declare bankruptcy and rewrite its collective bargaining agreements if a settlement could not be reached. Its offer to AMFA that was eventually accepted was described by the union's leadership as "the worst contract in the history of airline labor" (Brenner 2006, 2). Under its terms, the strikers would be rehired and then immediately laid off. The airline agreed not to contest unemployment benefit claims, offered to pay 4 weeks of severance pay and keep the former strikers on a recall list (Northwest Airlines Inc. and Aircraft Mechanics Fraternal Association 2006). AMFA tried to mount a "corporate campaign" aimed at embarrassing the Northwest Board of Directors but was unsuccessful because it had no allies, having such poor relations with other unions.

---

[18] For details of the AMFA negotiations and strike at Northwest, see Isidore (2005), Northwest CEO (2005), Maynard and Peters (2005), Brenner (2006), and Pongrace (2006).

[19] AMFA won the bargaining rights for workers represented by the International Association of Machinists at Northwest in 1999. For a review of AMFA's brief history (founded in 1962) and its outspoken leadership, see Rybak and Kennedy (2001).

The dispute between Northwest and AMFA and the 2004 California grocery strike, described earlier, were the twin landmarks of the new collective bargaining because of their length, the number of workers involved, and the employers' aggressiveness. Concluded: "The Northwest battle is being closely watched … as the labor movement finds itself at a crossroads, trying to stem several decades of declining membership across broad areas of the workforce, as well as internal divisiveness…. Many think a clear victory by the airline could result in more aggressive tactics by companies." Commentators even suggested that the union might have been goaded into its unsuccessful strike so that the strikers would be replaced, and the company could demonstrate its militancy for subsequent negotiations with other unions (Maher and Appel 2005).

The Detroit Symphony Orchestra: Saving the Orchestra or Serving the People?

In August 2010, negotiations between the Detroit Symphony Orchestra and the union of its musicians collapsed, and a 6-month strike began.[20] The employer demanded that the union accept deep wage cuts and a two-tier wage system. The union offered to take an initial wage cut but only if there were wage increases in later years of a collective agreement. After negotiating for months, management and union were quite close; the employer had increased the cost of its offer to $34 million over 3 years and the musicians lowered the cost of theirs to about $38 million. Management then increased their offer to $36 million which included $2 million earmarked by donors for community outreach and education. Bargaining broke down when the musicians insisted that all or most of the $2 million be used for salary increases.

The musicians were concerned that the pay cuts would destroy the orchestra by making it less appealing to present and potential members, allowing it to fall from its ranking as one of the top ten American orchestras. With lowered pay, musicians would start to audition for other orchestras. They also saw management's approach to bargaining as something that might spread to other orchestras in financial trouble. Management, it was argued, did not fully appreciate the quality of the musicians, and why they deserved higher pay (Boehm 2011).

Management argued that anything less than their demands for pay cuts would lead them to dissolve the orchestra (Smith 2010). The orchestra had projected losses of $9 million for 2010 and its endowment had fallen by nearly half its value since

[20] The negotiations and strike at the Detroit Symphony are described in: Detroit symphony musicians targeted (2010), Hogle (2010), Karoub (2010), Oestreich (2010), Smith (2010), Stryker (2010), Wakin (2011), Boehm (2011), Detroit orchestra back for encore after labor, budget discord (2011), and Johnson (2011).

2005 (Detroit Symphony 2010; Stryker 2010). Management said that it wanted to operate with a new performance model that shifted priorities from traditional concerts to community service. The musicians claimed that that they were already fulfilling their community service role with tours and educational programs (Johnson 2011). In prior negotiations there had also been temporary wage cuts but now the cuts would have to be permanent. The local economy of Detroit was in shambles, management argued, with a declining endowment, ticket sales, and donations; the symphony could not spend more money than it takes in. It had to pay off $58 million in loans and its endowment had fallen to $19 million from $80 million a decade earlier. The management of the Symphony claimed that their proposal as simply living within their means and adjusting the symphony to the needs and condition of its community. But the musicians thought management's demands would destroy a world-class orchestra.

In April 2011, the union and management reached a settlement. The musicians agreed to have their minimum salary cut by 25 %, and the number of permanent musicians reduced from 96 to 81 (Wakin 2010). The primary reason for the musicians approving the agreement was that it did not include a two-tier salary system.

Harley-Davidson: Moving On Down the Road to Concessions

Harley-Davidson, the iconic motorcycle maker, began its 2010 negotiations with union locals of the Steelworkers and the Machinists with threats to cut jobs.[21] If the unions at the two Wisconsin plants did not agree to major wage and work rule concessions aimed at cutting costs, the company would transfer work out of the state. (Ironically, the Harley-Davidson Museum was among Milwaukee's top tourist destinations and the company was a long-time source of civic pride in the city, so much so that its motorcycles were often nicknamed "Milwaukee Iron.") In September 2010, a tentative contract was presented to the workforces in Milwaukee area plants, along with company threats of shifting operations to the company's York, Pennsylvania plant where there had been earlier layoffs. Union leaders unanimously recommended that the union membership approve the new contract.

The long, 7-year agreement was approved by a vote of 53 % to 47 %. Wages were frozen for the entire contract. Nine-hundred full-time jobs (of 1,350) were kept at the two plants, but 150–250 casual workers would be hired to cover vacations, absences, and seasonal spikes in demand (demand for motorcycles spikes in the

[21] For details of the concession bargaining at Harley-Davidson see Clark (2010), Garrett (2010), Harley Davidson Milwaukee unions… (2010), and Ramde (2010).

spring and early summer). The hourly wage of regular workers ranged from $30.50 to $38.04, while that of the casual workers was $16.80 to $25.74.

The wage freeze was agreed to by the unions because they feared plant closings.[22] It was estimated that the collective agreement would produce annual savings of about $50 million per year for the company which was having difficulty adjusting to the recessions and international competition. A second wage tier had been created for the casual workers—a capitulation of the union to management's demands. As a union officer described the settlement: "The company stuck to their agenda and we ended up accepting their agenda. …This is absolutely a surrender for labor" (Uchitelle 2010, 1).

Mercury Marine: Threatening to Leave, Again

In Fond du Lac, Wisconsin, Mercury Marine, a well-known maker of marine engines and a division of Brunswick Corporation, bargained for concessions in 2009. It threatened to move production operations to lower-cost cities (Stillwater, Oklahoma or Kansas City, Missouri) if the union, the International Association of Machinists, did not accept such concessions as a 7-year wage freeze for current workers and a 30 % pay cut for laidoff workers called back to work (Dennis 2009). Nine hundred hourly workers at Mercury voted to reject the terms but 11 days later they voted again and accepted the agreement after the company announced it might be closing some operations. Under the terms of the new agreement, a two-tier wage system would be created. Workers who were laid off and then recalled would receive the wages of the lower tier rather than their old rate of pay (Uchitelle 2010). In the words of a Fond du Lac city councilor, the workers approving the agreement had a fundamental choice: "Ultimately it comes down to this, do they want a job or don't they want a job…." (Dennis 2009, 1).[23]

[22] Despite the settlement, there would still be mass layoffs among the regular workforce. By the end of 2011, Harley-Davidson announced that it was planning to lay off 250 workers or 25 % of the workers at its Milwaukee-area engine and parts plants. If there weren't sufficient "voluntary layoffs" by April 2012, the company would implement an involuntary layoff program. By that time, the company also planned to hire 150–250 seasonal workers (Harley-Davidson seeks voluntary layoffs 2011).

[23] In a similar vein, one worker who voted for the contract at Mercury Marine has reported "The economy is bad and we all got to take cuts. We got to give a little" (Fond Du Lac 2000). In the first quarter of 2011, sales increased at Mercury Marine, up 17 % from a year ago (Stanek 2011).

Cessna, and the Agreement by Default

Cessna Aircraft Co., America's largest builder of corporate jets, negotiated for wage and benefit concessions with the International Association of Machinists in 2010. Under the union's procedures, strikes must be approved by a two-thirds vote of the membership. If a strike is not approved, the members must accept the contract by default (McMillan 2010b). In this way, the workers at Cessna backed into a contract with major concessions.

The Cessna workers were worried about possible job losses, and with good reason. The machinists represented 2,300 hourly workers at the company's Wichita plant, down from 6,200 at the last negotiations 3 years ago (McMillan 2010a). One industry analyst commented on the impact of the financial crisis on Cessna as a major producer of business jets: "...during the recession ... wealthy individuals and corporations stopped buying aircraft and orders from fractional ownership companies dried up" (Lerner 2011, 1). Also, the company faced stiff competition internationally (from Embraer in Brazil) and nationally (from Hawker Beechcraft).

When the Cessna workers failed to approve of a strike, they accepted by default a 7-year contract with no automatic wage increases and only some minor increases in health care benefits. They were still concerned, however, that the company might move work elsewhere—the contract only guaranteed that the company would keep the final assembly of Citation business jets in Wichita. One union member, explaining why members did not vote to go on strike, explained the hopelessness of the present situation at the aircraft maker: "You've got to take what you can get now and fight another day." (McMillan 2010b, 1). Later that year, Textron, Cessna's parent company, announced that in the recession there had been no improvement in business jet orders and 700 workers would be laid off. The head of Cessna described the problem: "Cessna's performance continues to mirror the lackluster economy.... We must continue to lower our cost structure to remain competitive." (Marsh 2010, 1).[24] There were reports that other small aircraft producers, in particular Hawker Beechcraft, were eying the Cessna settlement and considering demanding similar concessions when it negotiates (Diffin 2010).[25]

---

[24] A year earlier, Cessna announced 1,300 new layoffs. The workforce had been cut in half during the recession (1300 new layoffs at Cessna Aircraft 2009).

[25] In October 2010, the Machinists union at Hawker Beechcraft ratified a 7-year agreement with a 10 % wage cut and guarantees that the company would not relocate its operations (Hawker Beechcraft machinists vote on new contract 2010).

Motts: A New Twist on Ultra Concession Bargaining

At the Mott's apple juice plant in Williamson, New York (about 60 miles west of Syracuse) the employer, Dr. Pepper/Snapple Group, demanded that 300 production workers, unionized by the United Food and Commercial Workers, accept a wage cut of $1.50 per hour, a freeze in their pensions, and no pensions for new hires. The company did, however, offer a $1,000 signing bonus.[26]

Despite its demands for concessions, Motts was profitable, reporting record profits of $555 million in 2009 and increasing its stock dividends by two-thirds. Motts argued that its workers were receiving an average of $21 per hour while the other food industry workers in that area were making $14 per hour. In other words, the concessions were needed simply because they were good for business.

Motts tried to justify its demand for concessions by arguing that as a public company it had an obligation to act in the best interests of all constituencies and therefore it should strive to be as profitable as possible. After striking for 16 weeks, the workers voted (by 185 for and 62 against) to return to work. Under the new 3-year collective agreement, pensions for present workers would not be frozen, as management had demanded, but newly hired workers would not participate in the regular pension but a separate defined-payment plan instead. Wages would be frozen but not cut as management had proposed. There would be a $1,000 signing bonus, and the company would pay for 80 % of the costs of health care benefits.

The strike had attracted national attention because a profitable company was demanding concessions in bargaining solely to improve its competitive position. A review of the dispute concluded: "Labor unions nationwide paid close attention to the strike, fearing that if Dr. Pepper/Snapple [Mott's parent company] were able to push through substantial cuts in wages and benefits that would embolden other profitable companies to do likewise. Traditionally, American companies have sought wage cuts only when they or the workers' plants were losing money or they were having a hard time competing with lower-cost competitors." (Greenhouse 2010b, 1).[27]

---

[26] For details on the Motts negotiation and strike, see AFL-CIO (2010), Greenhouse (2010a, b), and Groom (2010).

[27] In the first quarter of 2011, Dr. Pepper Snapple Group Inc. reported an increases in earnings per share and net sales (Dr. Pepper Snapple Group Inc. reports 7 percent net sales gain in first quarter 2011).

The Upheaval: Wisconsin and Its Public Workers

In one of the most bitter labor disputes in American history, the governor of Wisconsin, Scott Walker, a newly elected Republican, threatened unions of the state workers in February 2011.[28] Walker and the Republicans controlled the Wisconsin Assembly and Senate, and they proposed legislation that, among other measures, would prohibit collective bargaining over issues other than wages (e.g., work rules and pensions) and require unions to win back their bargaining certification annually. Walker also insisted that public employees increase their contributions to health care plans and pension plans.[29] The unions responded by offering some concessions—greater worker contributions to pension and health care plans (equal to a pay cut of 7 %)—but these were dismissed by Governor Walker as insufficient.

The governor's attempt to not only impose concessions in health care and pension plans but also restrict the bargaining power of public employee unions was viewed as overreaching. There was a huge uproar—thousands of unionized workers and their supporters (as many as 70,000 demonstrators on some days) from Wisconsin and other states marched on the state capital in Madison for 3 weeks. Democrats in the Senate fled the state to prevent the legislature from having the quorum needed to vote on the bill. In the meantime, the state assembly approved the bill. The demonstrations continued for 3 weeks. Much of the furor was because unions around the country feared that the limitations imposed on collective bargaining in the Wisconsin legislation would spread to other states with big budget deficits (e.g., Ohio, Indiana, Tennessee, Michigan, and Idaho, among others, had proposed union-limiting laws) (Greenhouse 2011a, b, c, d; Provance 2011; Williams 2011; Wisniewski 2010).[30]

---

[28] For descriptions of the union–public employer confrontation in Wisconsin, see Bauer (2011), Cooper and Greenhouse (2011), Davey (2011a, b), Greenhouse (2011a, b, d), Kelleher (2011), Lewis (2011), Malone (2011), Niquette (2011), Pitsch (2011), Provance (2011), Smith and Haberman (2011), Wheaton (2011), and Zernike and Saulny (2011).

[29] Public safety workers (police and firefighters) were exempted from the proposed law, and would pay only half the rate of the other public workers toward health care benefits and little or nothing toward their pensions. Public safety workers were excluded because the governor believed that they would lose support if it covered workers who enjoyed strong public support (Niquette 2011). Under the proposed bill, state employees, other than public safety workers, would have to contribute 5.8 % of their salaries toward their pensions (up from very little or nothing in many cases), and at least 12.6 % of their health care benefits (up from an average of 6 %) (Maher and Merrick 2011).

[30] In Ohio, legislation similar to that of Wisconsin was also passed by the state legislature and signed by the governor but it was rescinded by a voter referendum in November 2011. An important difference between the two laws is that the Ohio law included firefighters and police officers, groups excluded from the Wisconsin legislation. Opponents of the Ohio law could charge that it would negatively affect staffing in protective services (Niquette and Rosenkrantz 2011).

The Republicans in the Wisconsin state senate voted on a modified version of the bill that was stripped of sections appropriating funds; by doing so they had managed to bypass the requirement that the absent Democrats be present to constitute a quorum. The new bill limited collective bargaining to wages (excluding benefits), imposed a ceiling on negotiated wage increases equal to the increase in the Consumer Price Index, required public employee unions to be recertified by employee vote every year, and eliminated the automatic dues check-off. The bill was approved by the state assembly after some of its supporters were challenged in recall elections, and after it was temporarily blocked in the courts by its opponents (Davey 2011a; Paulson 2011; Riccardi 2011; Sulzberger and Tavernise 2011).

The confrontation in Wisconsin demonstrated the depth of the crisis for the American labor movement. Government employers were now going beyond ultra-concession bargaining to a campaign of blatant union suppression (Lewis 2011). The Wisconsin governor, facing a budget deficit of $3.6 billion in 2013, spoke of cost-cutting through collective bargaining as something that was not only desirable but crucial to the operation of his state's government. He claimed that he was trying to weaken public sector unions so communities would not have to confront powerful union opponents in the future and could better manage budget cuts. The unions responded by offering a few concessions and accusing the governor of "union busting."[31] The public agreed that workers' rights to union membership and bargaining should be protected, but also that the public employees of Wisconsin should share in the sacrifices already being made by private sector workers who were laid off or had their wages cut or frozen. In Wisconsin, we saw a potent mix of ultra-concession bargaining and union suppression, an attempt not only to achieve cost-cutting in bargaining but also to weaken unions as bargaining agents as well.[32] The governor had gone a step further than company negotiators.

The wave of ultra-concessionary bargaining in the private and public sectors over the past decade has a special edge to it. Employers saw an opportunity to lower labor costs by pressing for concessions and they used this opportunity to the fullest (Uchitelle 2010). This was not the usual collective bargaining in which negotiations might be tough and strikes might even occur, and in which the parties believed they could advance their mutual interests (Cutcher-Gershenfeld 2011). Instead one party, the employer, was clearly on the offensive, and the other, the union, bargained defensively to preserve past gains.

[31] President Obama characterized the Walker bill as an assault on unions (Greeley 2011).

[32] While public attention seemed fixated on the upheaval in Wisconsin, the legislature in Ohio passed legislation that was even more antiunion. The Ohio law banned health care benefits from bargaining, included firefighters and police, and allowed cities and school boards to impose their own final offers on unions if there were impasses in collective bargaining. The Ohio law did not survive a voter referendum (Maher and Nicas 2011; Union bashing 2011). One of the important side effects of the state-level attempts to restrict the bargaining rights of public employees has been the movement of union political funds to fight antiunion legislation and launch recall votes, and away from the presidential and congressional elections. Protecting bargaining rights became the highest political priority of labor unions (Trottman and Mullins 2012).

The first wave of concession bargaining in the 1980s created the conditions for second wave. With the decline of the labor accord during the first wave, the key assumptions of concession bargaining—employer credibility, the quid pro quo, and the not-to-be-repeated trait—lost their relevancy. Even in the auto industry, where the labor accord was an well-documented historical accommodation between labor and management, the companies argued that their competiveness was hampered by the gap between union and nonunion wages and benefits, and that in today's world job security could never be guaranteed no matter how much the workers sacrificed. The first wave of concession bargaining started the transformation of union–management relations in the United States; the second wave entrenched a tough, new way of bargaining—an ultra-concession bargaining.

References

AFL-CIO (2010) http://www.aflcio.org. 9 September. Accessed 9 September 2010.

America's other auto industry (2008) Wall Street Journal. 1 December: A22.

Applebone P (2011) Connecticut steps closer to mass layoffs as the union's next move is awaited. New York Times. 1 July: A20

Bagli CV (2011) Civic group says that concessions are needed from construction unions. New York Times 25 May: A19.

Bailey J (2006) Northwest attendants agree to concessions as pilots continue talks. New York Times. 2 March: C1.

Bauer S (2011) Wisconsin lawmakers to take up bill to cripple unions. http://www.newsyahoo.com 24 February. Accessed 24 February 2011.

Becker SE (1981) The bankruptcy law's effect on collective bargaining agreements. Columbia Law Review 81: 391–409.

Bluestone B (2011) Fiscal crisis and the future of public unions. Perspectives on work. 15: 6–8.

Boehm M (2011) Detroit Symphony strike prompts discussion of what's fair pay for symphony musicians. Los Angeles Times. http://www.latimes.com. 24 February. Accessed 1 March 2011.

Brenner M (2006). Airline Workers United forms to fight concessions industry-wide. Labor Notes. http://www.labornotes.com 8 January. Accessed 30 March 2011.

Brownfield A (2011) Ohio safety forces study shows union concessions. Bloomberg Businessweek. http://www.businessweek.com. 18 October. Accessed 18 October 2011.

Bunkley N (2007) Auto workers make major concessions, including pay cuts, at Delphi, large parts supplier. New York Times http://www.nytimes.com 30 June. Accessed 15 May 2011.

Bunkley N (2011a) Ford plans to hire more than 7,000 workers. New York Times. http://www.nytimes.com 2 January. Accessed 10 January 2011

Bunkley N (2011b) Resurgent G.M. posts 2010 profit of $4.7 billion. New York Times 25 February: C1

Bunkley N (2011c) Smaller cars lift Ford's profit to $2.55 billion. New York Times. http://www.nytimes.com 27 April. Accessed 28 April 2011,

Carey S, Nicas J (2012) AMR seeks to cut 15% of jobs. Wall Street Journal 2 February: B1

Chaison G (2006) Unions in American. Sage. Thousand Oaks, CA.

Chaison G (2007) Airline collective bargaining and the return of concessionary bargaining. J. Labor Res. 28: 642–657.

Cho D, Goldfarb ZA (2008) UAW vows to fight salary concessions. Washington Post. http://www.washingtonpost.com. 24 December. Accessed 15 March 2011.

Cho D, Mufson D (2008) Bush to steer course of and to automakers: managed bankruptcy raised as one option. Washington Post. 19 December: A1.

Chon et al. (2012) Rivals eye American Airlines. Wall Street Journal 13 January: A1, A4.

Chrysler (2009) Chrysler restructuring plan for long-term viability. http://www.chrysler.com. 17 February. Accessed 30 March 2011.

Chupaska S (2011) Waterford school board oks $42.9M budget. http://www.theday.com (Connecticut) http://www.theday.com. 28 January. Accessed 28 January 2011.

Cieply M (2011) Hollywood labor fight looms as money for benefits wanes. New York Times http://www.nytimes.com. 27 November. Accessed 27 November 2011.

Clark A (2010) Harley-Davidson unions back deal. The Guardian. http://www.guardian.com 14 September. Accessed 14 September 2010.

Cooper M (2007) Southern California grocery workers vote massive strike. The Nation http://www.thenation.com. 25 June. Accessed 1 March 2011.

Cooper M, Greenhouse S (2011) Unions debate what to give to save bargaining. New York Times. February 27:A1.

Cooper M, Walsh MW (2011) Governments consider cuts to once untouchable pensions. New York Times http://www.nytimes.com 26 May. Accessed 26 May 2011.

Cutcher-Gershenfeld J (2011) Moving beyond confrontations over public sector collective bargaining. Employment Policy Research Network http://www.employmentpolicy.org 24 March. Accessed 24 March 2011.

Davey S (2011a) Wisconsin court reinstates law on union rights. New York Times http://www.nytimes.com 15 June. Accessed 16 June 2011

Davey M (2011b) Wisconsin senate limits bargaining by public workers. New York Times 9 March: 1, 14.

Delany S (2011) Sterling Heights, firefighters agree to wage concessions. Advisor and Source http://www.sourcenewspapers.com 5 May. Accessed 5 May 2011.

De La Merced D (2011) American Airlines Parent Files for Bankruptcy. New York Times http://www.nytimes.com 29 November. Accessed 29 November 2011.

Dennis L (2009) City and state officials not giving up on Mercury Marine deal. WUWM http://www.wuwm.com 25 April. Accessed 26 April 2011.

Detroit orchestra back for encore after labor, budget discord. (2011) PBS Newshour http://www.pbsnewshour.org 11 April. Accessed 20 October 2011.

Detroit, the union and improving times. (2011) New York Times. http://www.nytimes.com 28 July. Accessed 1 August 2011.

Detroit Symphony musicians targeted for deep slashes: Will other symphony orchestra musicians also be under the gun? (2010). http://www.prnewswire.com. 29 July. Accessed 30 July 2010.

Diffin S (2010) Labor expert: Cessna decision could impact Hawker offer. KAKE. http://www.kake.com 20 September. Accessed 1 March 2011.

Dolan M (2011a). Michigan sizes up taking over Flint. Wall Street Journal. 10 November: A5

Dolan M (2011B) UAW moves more swiftly on foreign auto plants. Wall Street Journal. 9 December: B3

Dolan M (2012) Humbled Flint forced to take state's orders. Wall Street Journal 18 January: A2.

Dr. Pepper Snapple Group, Inc. reports 7 percent net sales gain in first quarter. (2011) http://www.vendingmarketwatch.com. 1 May. Accessed May 25, 2011.

Durbin D, Krisher T (2011) US auto sales rise in 2010, but remain below highs. Daily News (Memphis) http://www.memphisdailynews.com 5 January. Accessed 6 January 2011.

Dziczek K et al. (2008) Beyond the big leave: The future of U.S. automotive human resources. Center for Automotive Research, Ann Arbor Michigan.

Feldacker B (2000) Labor guide to labor law, 4th edition, Prentice Hall, Upper Saddle River, NJ.

Finamore C (2007) Airline bankruptcies, mergers and profits provoke unions. Labornet http://www.labornet.org. Accessed 27 February 2012.

Foskett, Jr. SH (2011) In Worcester, health savings allow schools to avoid layoffs. Worcester Telegram & Gazette http://www.telegram&gazette.com 12 July. Accessed 12 July 2011.

Fond Du Lac/Mercury Marine union oks concessions on third vote (2000). St. Paul Pioneer Press. http://www.twincities.com 5 September. Accessed 9 June 2011.
Garrett J (2010) Harley-Davidson to remain Wisconsin-made. New York Times, http://www.nytimes.com. 14 September. Accessed 25 May 2011.
Gerdano SJ (2012) The future of collective bargaining under bankruptcy: The brave new world facing the old economy industries. The American Bankruptcy Institute. http://www.abiworld.org 15 February. Accessed 15 February 2012.
Greeley B (2011) Why we should debate public-sector bargaining. Bloomberg. http://www.bloomberg.com. 24 February. Accessed 23 January 2012.
Greenhouse S (2003a) An airline avoids bankruptcy: concessions. New York Times April 26: 3
Greenhouse S (2003b). Unions find that employers want more concessions. New York Times. 11 July: 12.
Greenhouse S (2010a) Ending strike, Mott's plant union accepts deal. New York Times http://www.nytimes.com 13 June. Accessed 13 June.
Greenhouse S (2010b) In Mott's strike, more than pay at stake. New York Times, http://www.nytimes.com 17 August. Accessed 18 August 2010.
Greenhouse S (2011a) In Indiana, clues to the future of Wisconsin labor, New York Times 26 February: 1, 25.
Greenhouse S (2011b) Ohio's anti-union law is tougher than Wisconsin's. New York Times. 1 April: A16.
Greenhouse S (2011c) Strained states turning to laws to curb labor unions. New York Times. 4 January: A1.
Greenhouse S (2011d) Strikers trade barbs with Verizon. New York Times. http://www.nytimes.com 12 August. Accessed 12 August 2011.
Greenhouse S (2011e) A water-shed moment for public-sector unions. New York Times http://www.nytimes. 18 February. Accessed 18 February 2011.
Groom, DJ (2010) Mott's strike ends in Williamson as union approves contract. The Syracuse Post-Standard http://www.syracuse.com. 13 September. Accessed 13 September 2010.
Gustafson C (2012) Report: Some pension costs improving. San Diego Union Tribune. http://www.utsandiego.com 28 February. Accessed 29 February 2012.
Harley Davidson Milwaukee unions accept concession laden contract. (2010) Fox43. http://fox43.com. 13 September. Accessed 1 March 2011.
Harley-Davidson seeks voluntary layoffs (2011). Powersports Business. http://www.powersports-business.com. 23 December. Accessed 21 February 2012.
Hawker Beechcraft machinists vote on new contract (2010). ABC News http://www.abcnews.com 16 October. Accessed 31 July 2010.
Headapohl J (2011). UAW official: Chrysler may add up to 3,000 jobs. http://www.mlive.com. 12 May. Accessed 12 May 2011.
Higgins T (2012) G.M. earns a record $9.19 billion net income. Bloomberg News http://www.bloomberg.com 16 February. Accessed 16 February 2012.
Hirsch B (2007) Unions and wages in the US airline industry. IATA Economics. http://www.iata.org. July. Accessed 29 February 2012.
Hirsch J (2012) Losses in Europe and Asia hurt Ford's fourth-quarter profit. Los Angeles Times http://www.latimes.com 27 January. Accessed 28 June 2012.
Hogle P (2010) DSO future viability. Pierce County Herald. http://www.piercecountyherald.com. 2 September. Accessed 2 September 2010.
Huffstutter, PJ (2011) Ralphs, Vons, Albertsons, union reach labor deal, avert strike. Los Angeles Times http://www.latimes.com. 20 September. Accessed 20 September 2011.
Isidore C (2005) Northwest flies through strike. CNN Money. http://www.money.cnn.com. 22 August. Accessed 30 March 2011.
Jakab S (2012) Blowout car sales will shift to lower gear. Wall Street Journal. 1 February 2012: C1
Johnson L B (2011) DSO may emerge as a vastly different organization. Detroit News http://www.detnews.com 22 February. Accessed 22 February.

Kaplan T (2011) Another union yields on pay agreement with New York. New York Times 17 July: 16
Katz, HC et al. (2002) Autos: Continuity and Change in Collective Bargaining. In Clark, P F et al. (2002) Collective bargaining in the private sector. Champaign Urbana, University of Illinois, Industrial Relations Research Association. 55–90
Karoub J (2010) Budget Woes Sowing Discord at Detroit Orchestra, Associated Press, 31 August.
Kelleher J (2011) Wisconsin lawmakers agree to advance budget debate. Chicago Tribune 24 February. Accessed 25 February 2011.
Kittilstad J (2011) Proposed wage freeze for MN teachers passes first hurdle. Fox21 online. http://www.fox21online.com. 25 January. Accessed 23 January 2011.
Koenig D (2012) American Airlines seek 20 pct in labor costs. Bloomberg Businessweek. http://www.businessweek.com. 1 February. Accessed 3 February 2012.
Krisher T (2008) Automakers struggle to survive past mistakes. AP news release. http://www.ap.com. 1 November 2008. Accessed 15 February 2010.
Kutalik C (2007) Automakers push VEB solution for industry crisis. Labor Notes. http://www labornotes.com. October. Accessed 30 October 2011.
Lahart J (2012) American needs merger flight plan. Wall Street Journal 9 February: C10
Lerner J (2011) Head of Cessna Aircraft retires. Financial Times. http//www.ft.com. 3 May. Accessed 26 May 2011.
Lewis F (2011) Wisconsin highlights union fight. Congressional Quarterly http://www.congress.org. 14 March. Accessed 14 March 2011.
Maher K, Merrick A (2011) Wisconsin Democrats push alternative plan. Wall Street Journal http://www.wsj.com 24 February. Accessed 24 February 2011.
Maher K, Appel T (2005) Union weakness lets firm seek big concessions. Wall Street Journal. http://www.wsj.com 19 September. Accessed 30 March 2011.
Maher K, Nicas J (2011) Power of unions tested in Ohio vote. Wall Street Journal. http://www.wsj.com. 9 November: A4
Malone J (2011) Union power at issue in Wisconsin dispute. Voice of America news. http://www.voanews.org 24 February. Accessed 23 February 2012.
Marks A (2005) Why big labor hasn't aided striking machinists. Christian Science Monitor. http://www.csm.com 29 August. Accessed 29 August 2005.
Marsh AK (2010) Cessna to reduce workforce by 700. Aircraft Owners and Pilots Association. http://www.aopa.org.html. 21 September. Accessed 6 February 2012.
Masters et al. (2010) The state of public sector unionism: Challenges and opportunities. Employ. Respons. Rights J. 22:255–274.
Maynard M (2003a) Delta and pilots start talks on concessions. New York Times. 5 December. http://www.nytimes.com. 5 December. Accessed 10 December 2010.
Maynard M (2003b) The end of Detroit: How the big three lost their grip on the American car market. Doubleday, New York.
Maynard, M (2004a) Delta pilots vote to accept 32.5 percent pay cut. New York Times 12 November: C3.
Maynard M (2004b) Pilots union agrees to cuts at Northwest. New York Times 15 October: C4
Maynard M (2004c) US Airways sets deadline for concessions New York Times. 3 September: 2
Maynard M, Bunkley N (2006) Parts supplier reaches buyout deal with U.A.W. New York Times 10 June: C1
Maynard M, Peters JW (2005) Strike is called by mechanics for Northwest. New York Times. 20 August: A1
McKersie R. (2011) Public sector labor relations: A system struggling to adjust to the financial crisis. Perspectives on Work. 15: 3–5.
McMillan M (2010a) Cessna, Machinists negotiations aren't about 'two warring sides'. 20 August. Accessed 7 February 2011.
McMillan M (2010b) Cessna strike would have hurt economy. Kansas City Star http://www.kansas.com. 20 September. Accessed 20 September 2010.

Mewes T (2011) School district employees brace for possible wage freeze. Daily Herald (Austin). http://www.austindailyherald.com. 27 January. Accessed 7 March 2011.

Michels J. (2008) Economist: Labor unions face uphill battle. Aviation Week. http://www.aviationweek.com. 10 January. Accessed 27 February 2012.

Mitchell D.J.B. (2010) Government by (hot) checks and (im)balances: California's state budget from the May 2009 voter rejection to the October 2010 budget deal. Unpublished manuscript, UCLA Anderson Graduate School.

Moody E. (2011) Dallas School District, teachers reach contract. http://www.citizensvoice.com 12 May. Accessed 12 May 2011.

Naughton K, Lippert J (2011) UAW said to seek early labor agreements with GM, Ford, Chrysler. http://www.bloomberg.com. 20 April. Accessed 6 February 2012.

Nicas J, Spector M (2011) AMR and pilots prep for talks. Wall Street Journal 1 December: B1

Niquette M (2011) Walker's bill gives Wisconsin police a pass on pension payments. http://www.bloomberg.com 25 February. Accessed 25 February 2011.

Niquette M, Rosenkrantz H (2011) Ohio ballot win for unions may not mean end of labor fights. http://www.businessweek.com 10 November. Accessed 10 November 2010.

No S. Calif. grocery strike: workers approve deal. (2011) Bloomberg Businessweek. 24 September. Accessed 24 September 2011.

Northwest Airlines (2005) Northwest issues statement on AMFA decision to 'discontinue' negotiations. Aero News Network. http://www.nwa.com 13 September. Accessed 1 September 2011.

Northwest Airlines, Inc. and Aircraft Mechanics Fraternal Association (2006) Strike Settlement Agreement. Unpublished. 9 October 2006.

Oestreich JR (2010) Detroit Symphony players reject contract proposals. New York Times, http://www.nytimes.com. 29 August. Accessed 30 August 2011.

Pew Charitable Trusts (2009) Layoffs, furloughs and union concessions: The prolonged and painful process of balancing city budgets. http://www.pewtrusts.org. 22 September. Accessed 6 February 2012.

Paulson A (2011) Wisconsin recall elections begin a legacy of Scott Walker's labor union wars. Christian Science Monitor. 12 July. Accessed 13 July 2011.

Perez-Pena R (2011) In New Jersey, law makers curb worker benefits. New York Times. 24 June: A1.

Pettit CA (2008) CRS report for congress: Rejection of collective bargaining agreements in Chapter 11 bankruptcies. Washington D.C.: Congressional Research Service, #RL34486.

Pitsch M (2011) Questions and answers about the new collective bargaining law. http://www.Madison.com 17 March. Accessed 17 March 2011.

Pongrace D (2006) Major work stoppages in 2004 and 2005. Compensation and Working Conditions Online. http://www.bls.gov 25 October. Accessed 5 February 2012.

Powell M (2011) Public workers facing outrage as budget crisis grows. New York Times 2 January 2011: A1.

Public-worker unions confront U.S. governors over benefits in role switch. (2011) http://www.bloomberg.com. 20 January. Accessed 20 January 2011.

Provance J (2011) Demonstrators protest Ohio labor law changes. Toledo Blade http://www.toledoblade.com 18 February. Accessed 5 February 2012.

Ramde D (2010) Harley, union reach proposed labor agreement. Associated Press http://www.google.com. 4 September. Accessed 4 September 2010.

Riccardi N (2011) Close vote: A Wisconsin judicial election: A usually quiet race become a referendum the Governor's battle with unions. Los Angeles Times April 26:2

Roberson J. (2012) GM books record annual profit; Union workers dues $7,000. USA Today. http://www.usatoday.com 16 February. Accessed 16 February 2012.

Rybak DC, Kennedy T (2001) Below the radar: union proudly depicts itself as different. Star Tribune (Minneapolis, MN) 1 March: 1D.

San Bernadino County firefighters accept pension cut (2011) Iepolitics. http://www. iepolitics.net. 15 April. Accessed 21 May 2012.

Schoen DE (2011) The union threat to the Democrat's future. Wall Street Journal. http://www.wsj.com. 20 January. Accessed 20 January 2011.

Shapiro L (2011) Detroit auto workers look to see scales balances with three back in black. Huffpost Business. http://www.huffingtonpost.com.html 20 May. Accessed 21 May 2011.
Smith T (2010) Potential strike at Detroit Symphony sends warning throughout orchestral world. Baltimore Sun. http://www.Baltimoresun.com. 30 August. Accessed 30 August 2010.
Smith B, Haberman M (2011) Labor faces a moment of truth. http://www.politico.com. 21 February. Accessed 21 February 2011.
Snavely B (2011) Chrysler workers narrowly ok deal after dramatic split in vote. Detroit Free Press. http://www.freep.com. 27 October. Accessed 30 October 2011.
Stanek H (2011) Sales up at Mercury Marine. The Northwestern (Oshkosh, MI) http://www.the.northwestern.com. 25 April. Accessed 25 May 2011.
Stoll JD (2009) What would happen if one or more of the Detroit auto makers went bankrupt?: Ten hard questions facing the 'car czar'. Wall Street Journal. 22 January: A12
Stryker M (2010) Final talk produces no DSO contract. Detroit Free Press, http://www.freep.com. 28 August. Accessed 5 February 2012.
Sulzberger AG, Tavernise S (2011) GOP senators in Wisconsin say they will resume work. New York Times. http://www.nytimes.com 22 February. Accessed February 22, 2011.
Suroweicki J (2011) State of the unions. The New Yorker. http://www.newyorker.com 17 January. Accessed 15 January 2012.
Terlep S (2012) Target at post-bailout GM: Earning $10 billion a year. Wall Street Journal 6 February: A1
1300 new layoffs at Cessna Aircraft. (2009). CBS News. http://www.cbsnews.com.html. 12 June. Accessed 7 February 2010.
Troianovski A (2011) Verizon pursues tough line on labor. Wall Street Journal 13 July: B1.
Trottman M, Mullin B (2012) Wall Street Journal. http://www.wsj.com. 27 February. Accessed 27 February 2012.
Tyson workers end strike (2004). New York Times. http://www.nytimes.com. 30 January. Accessed 21 May 2012.
Uchitelle L (2010) Unions yield on wage scales to preserve jobs. New York Times, 19 November: A1
Union bashing, now in Ohio. (2011) New York Times, 5 May: 22
Vlasic B (2011a) In its rebound Detroit focuses on selling smaller cars. http://www.nytimes.com 29 May: Accessed 30 May 2011.
Vlasic B (2011b) With new labor contracts, Detroit protects turnaround. http://www.nytimes.com 27 October. Accessed 27 October 2011.
Vlasic B (2011c) With source, GM stands auto-making on its head. http://www.nytimes.com 13 June. Accessed 13 June 2011.
Vail B (2012) Hostess, bankrupt maker of Twinkies and Wonder Bread, pushes major concessions on unions. In These Times. http://www.inthesetimes.com 31 January. Accessed 22 February 2012.
Vlasic B, Bunkley N (2008) GM says US cash is its best hope. http://www.nytimes.com. 8 November. Accessed 8 November 2011
Vitullo-Martin J and H Cohen (2011) Construction labor costs in New York City, Regional Plan Association, NY.
Wakin D (2010) Day of strike dawns for Detroit musicians. New York Times. http://www.nytimes.com 3 October. Accessed 6 February 2012.
Wakin D (2011) Detroit Symphony reaches deal with musicians. http://www.nytimes.com 8 April. Accessed 31 July 2011.
Walsh MW (2011a) A path is set for states to escape debt burdens. New York Times. 20 January: A1
Walsh MW (2011b) The little state with a big mess. New York Times. 22 October: BU1,6.
Weir T (2007) Tiers of grief: The double standard for Southern California supermarket workers was a good idea only in pregnancy. Grocery Headquarters 73:6.
Wheaton S (2011) Discord, state by state. New York Times 21 January:20.
Williams T (2011) The battle over union rights, state by state. New York Times. http://www.nytimes.com 6 February. Accessed 11 March 2011.

Wisniewski M (2010) Factbox: Several U.S. states consider union limits. Reuters. 6 February. Accessed 25 February 2012.

Woodall B (2011) Akerson-King meet, story and sum up of the talks to this point. Bernie.woodall@thomsonreuters.com. Personal e-mail message. 7 September.

Zernike K and S. Saulny (2011) Standoffs, protests and a prank call. New York Times, 24 February: A20.

Chapter 5
The Present and Future of Unions Settling for Less

Abstract I ask what the new collective bargaining means and whether it will last? I conclude that ultra-concession bargaining evolved from the declining size and influence of American unions and will become the way of the future in collective bargaining. I also recognize that ultra-concession bargaining can sometimes benefit unionized firms and their workers by making employers more competitive and saving jobs, though we do see some clearly negative consequences in the limits of collective bargaining as a way to promote and protect the workers' voice at the workplace.

Keywords Ultra-concession bargaining • Labor accord • Public sector bargaining • Collective bargaining coverage • Union decline

The famed labor reporter A.H. (Abe) Raskin once asked; "Can a labor movement dedicated to the pursuit of 'more' accommodate to the necessity of settling for less (Raskin 1982, 12)?" Unions now seem to have little choice but settle for less!

We have seen two waves of concession bargaining during which unions had to take steps backward. In this chapter we ask: What does the new collective bargaining mean? Is the new collective bargaining—this ultra-concession bargaining—the result or the cause of general union decline? And should we expect it to last?

First, we must recognize, for the sake of contrast, that recent concession bargaining is not confined to the United States. We have seen negotiations over wage, benefit, and work rule concessions in other countries where employers have been affected by the financial crisis and global competition. For example, in Canada, unions of both public and private sector workers have been on the defensive, trying to protect past gains and limit the outsourcing of jobs (Rose and Chaison 1996, 2001;

G. Chaison, *The New Collective Bargaining*, SpringerBriefs in Economics,
DOI 10.1007/978-1-4614-4024-6_5,

Hoffman 2009; Matas 2010).[1] Canadian unions have had to negotiate with US-based multinational companies that threaten to transfer work back home if concessions are not granted (Austen 2012a, b; Paddon 2012).[2] In Britain, a large and increasing number of employers have demanded wage freezes (Jones 2008). In Germany, a wide variety of pay and work rule concessions have been negotiated by employers threatening to relocate (Landler 2005; Massa-Wirth and Seifert 2005; Hassel 2010; Ewing 2011). In France, there has been a clear trend toward concession bargaining of all types (Carley et al. 2009). In Argentina, for example, the federal government demanded that public workers accept lower wages and blamed the unions for holding back an economic recovery (Romig 2011). But the ultra-concession bargaining that we see in the United States is so widespread and so intense that it is uniquely American. Unlike what is happening in other countries, the American strain of concession bargaining tells much more than what bargaining might look like in the wake of a financial crisis—its shows us the contours significant and, in all likelihood, permanently changed relationship between employers and unions.

In the United States, ultra-concession bargaining was created by a combination of emboldened employers and weakened unions. Chaison (2006) observed that employers have always been reluctant participants in collective bargaining; many employers considered bargaining to be an expensive burden, though one that they could live with if they absolutely had to. The labor accord, mentioned in the preceding two chapters, was a tacit understanding, a sense of accommodation between unions and employers that shaped much of the American labor relations landscape, and led to mutual acceptance at the bargaining table. But now the labor accord has faded away, and with it a framework of union–management accommodation. "Under intense competitive pressures, management retreated from its commitment to collective bargaining…" (Chaison and Bigelow 2002, 22). Employers now see bargaining as a forum for containing or reducing labor costs, for getting back what was once given. In the face of such pressure, for unions, winning in bargaining simply means not losing (Chaison 2006).[3]

American unions are now in a tenuous position and their declining bargaining coverage[4] has been both a cause and consequence of ultra-concession bargaining. In 2011, coverage under collective bargaining agreements stood at only 13.0 for all

[1] For example, Caterpillar announced in February 2012 that it would be closing a locomotive plant in London, Ontario, after locking out workers for a year. The company had demanded that the Canadian Auto Workers agree to a 50 % wage cut and substantial cuts in employee benefits and pensions. The plant employed 670 workers, whose work would be transferred to other facilities in North and South America (Austen 2012b).

[2] For US/Canadian comparisons of first wave concession bargaining (as wage freezes or reductions, lump-sum payments, and two-tier wage provisions) see Rose and Chaison (1996, 88). Concessions occurred more often in the United States (often at least twice as often as measured as a percent of settlements in 1981–1992).

[3] As dramatic indicator of rising employer opposition to unions nationally, there has been an increase in employer lockouts at impasses in bargaining (Greenhouse 2012).

[4] For a discussion of the use of collective bargaining coverage to measure union influence see Schmitt and Mitukiewicz (2011, 4). A comprehensive and cross-national review of the impact of collective bargaining coverage, including its link to bargaining power, is Traxler and Brandl (2009).

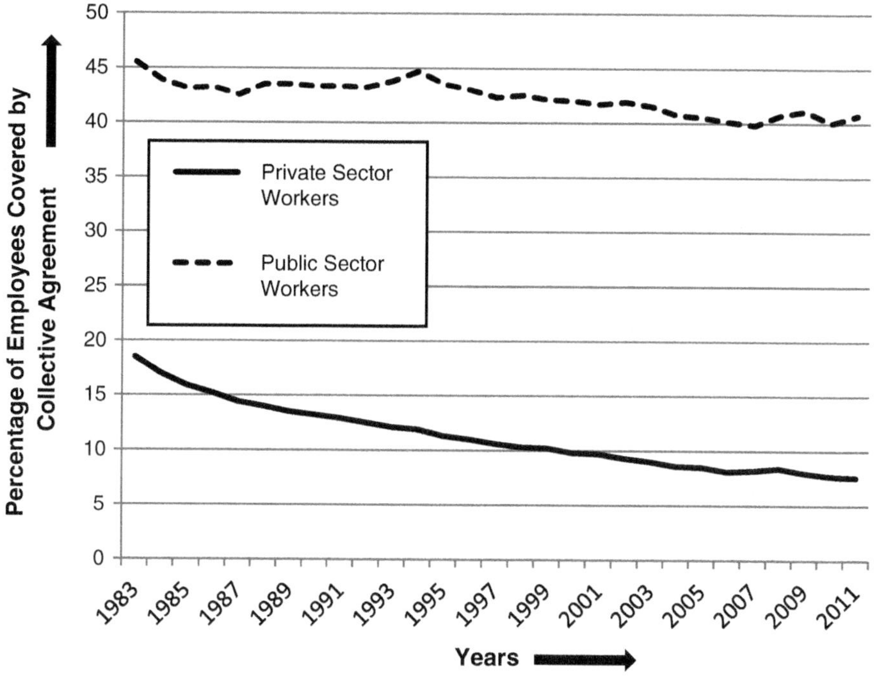

Fig. 5.1 Percentage of public and private sector workers covered by collective bargaining agreements, 1983–2011

workers. In the public sector, a large share of the workforce remained covered by collective agreements (40.7 %), most likely because public employers did not resist the unionization of their workforces and cannot relocate their operations or threaten to do so to stifle drives for unionization (Chaison and Rose 1991; Chaison 2006). In private employment, the collective bargaining coverage was only 7.6 % in 2011 (in other words, only about 1 in 12 workers in private employment is covered by a collective agreement). Bargaining coverage followed a long-term decline, particularly in the private sector (see Fig. 5.1). Collective bargaining coverage is even low in the traditional strongholds of unionism like transportation and utilities (22.1 % in 2011), manufacturing (11.2 %) construction (14.9 %), and mining (7.8 %).

Indeed there are no heavily unionized industries where a majority of workers are unionized. Even in the public sector, for every worker covered by a collective agreement there are nearly two who are not (Union membership and coverage in 2011 2011; United States Department of Labor 2012).[5]

[5] A major reason for the decline in collective bargaining coverage and union membership is the inability of unions to organize a sufficient number of new members to offset losses caused by mass layoffs and the transfer of work abroad in the industries of greater union presence (Chaison 2010). It would be difficult to exaggerate the extent to which American unions have declined in size and influence, and with it, bargaining power. As one observer succinctly summarized the situation "the United States has the smallest and most besieged union movement among advanced economies" (Reich 2012, 2).

With the low and declining collective bargaining coverage, unionized firms feel intense competitive pressures from the nonunion companies in their industries.[6] Employers find it risky to be one of the few higher-cost unionized firms in their industry and they use concession bargaining to compete by narrowing the gap between union and nonunion labor costs. This is a key objective of concession bargaining—*narrowing the gap*. In the third and fourth chapters, I wrote about the attempts to narrow the labor cost gaps between the older, legacy airlines and younger low-cost carriers in the airlines, and the gap between the Detroit Three automakers, all unionized, and the nonunion foreign carmakers.

When unions appear to be bargaining from weakness by bargaining backward, nonunion workers are naturally reluctant to opt for unionization.[7] Union organizing campaigns fail. The only way that unions can maintain their earlier organizing success rates (around 50–60 %) is by organizing less, that is, going forward only with those campaigns for which they feel that have the best chances of winning (Chaison 2006).

In other words, concession bargaining sullies the reputation of unions as bargaining agents, making bargaining seem like a losing deal in the eyes of nonunion workers.[8] There is an obvious vicious cycle here; declining collective bargaining coverage leads to ultra-concession bargaining, and ultra-concession bargaining leads to declining collective bargaining coverage (Chaison 2006). At the same time, as if to create as "perfect storm" of calamity for unions, the public support for unions is declining; the Gallup poll shows that in 2010 only 48 % of the general population approved of labor unions, compared to 59 % in 2008 (Tyler 2009). Declining public support for unions means that politicians feel more comfortable passing antiunion laws. Recall how the widespread public reaction against unions in Wisconsin emboldened legislators to draft antiunion laws and encouraged concession bargaining. And there was also ample scapegoating of unions in Congress' recent search for solutions to revive the economy in general and the auto industry in particular. Unionization was equated with high operating costs and lost jobs, and unions were characterized as special interest groups promoting their members welfare rather than the wages and working conditions of all workers. The attack was not only against unions but also against what unions do—collective bargaining.

Employers find little to lose and much to gain by fighting unions rather than accepting unions as equals in bargaining. They see unions as weakened and with declining public support, and so they turn to collective bargaining as a solution to

---

[6] As a result, union bargaining power, as measured by wage gains, tends to be low when there is low union bargaining coverage (Mishel 1986).

[7] In other words, the demand for unions would decrease if workers saw unions as less effective in winning and maintaining improved wages and working conditions whether such is caused by greater employer opposition, deregulation, or the declining ability to strike (Kaufman 2004).

[8] It might result in not only union defeats in union organizing drives but also the emergence of independent nonunion forms of worker representation (for example, representation through workplace joint consultation committees) that do not challenge employer control as does collective bargaining (e.g., Greenhouse 2011b).

their competitive challenges. Concession bargaining, employers believe, provides companies with lower costs and relief from work rules—a chance for restructuring and eventual profitability. And it greatly lightens the burden of being a unionized company adrift in a sea of nonunion competitors by narrowing the union–nonunion wage and benefit gap.

Is the new collective bargaining the way bargaining will be done from now on? Have the fundamental understandings underlying bargaining changed, never to return to the way they once were? Although it is always difficult to speculate about long-term trends in labor relations, the cycle of union decline, just discussed, strongly suggests that today's new bargaining will become tomorrow's bargaining as usual. Conventional collective bargaining will continue but it will be greatly diminished—most employers will push to control the bargaining agenda which greatly emphasizes their ability (or rather, their inability) to pay. The labor accord has faded away, accommodations based on mutual respect are now the exception and not the rule, and the lowered labor costs achieved in ultra-concession bargaining are obvious for all to see. Employers are only stopped from pushing for more and more concessions by their own doubts about whether more concessions would create true cost reductions. For example, employers may wonder if two-tier wage systems might eventually result in high turnover among embittered lower-tier workers (this happened in the California grocery industry). Do wage cuts and reduced job security through work rule changes make it too difficult to recruit and retain a workforce?[9] Employers will ask themselves: Do concessions really work?

What shape will the new ultra-concession bargaining take? First, we can expect the centers of concession bargaining, such as airlines and autos, to remain focused on lowering the gap between their labor costs and those of their nonunion competitors. (Even after the Detroit Three returned to profitability, remnants of concession bargaining remained in the form of two-tiered wage plans, lower wage increase matched with large lump-sum payments. In the airlines, pensions remained frozen after concession bargaining.) In the public sector, that new locus of ultra-concession bargaining, there will be increased pressure from the public for wage freezes or wages and job cuts. As their budgets are upset by the heavy costs of employee pension and health care plans in their collective agreements, public employers will try to bargain their ways through budgetary shortfalls (Baxter 2011; Cooper 2010; Maher 2011). By the end of 2010, public employers and the public at large were shocked by the tremendous debts of American states and cities, although there was no consensus whether the cure was higher taxes or cutting labor cost through concession bargaining, or both (Cooper 2010; Greenhouse 2011a; Maher 2011).

It could be argued that ultra-concession bargaining actually benefits unions in the long run because it enables unionized companies to survive, and so unions can retain their bargaining status and some union workers keep their jobs. For instance,

[9] For example, cutting public employee's pay and benefits to balance state budgets could in the long-term drive the best public employees into jobs in the private sector and thus lower the quality of government services, while also reducing consumer spending by public workers and cutting revenues from sales taxes (Maher 2011).

we saw such benefits in the apparently rebounding auto industry. In an editorial, the New York Times declared: "…Detroit automakers must remember that their rebound would not have been possible without deep concessions by the [UAW]" (Detroit, the union and improving times 2011, 1). Lee (2011), for example, observed how that "scaled-down" labor costs initiated by two-tier wage systems (in which the lower tier became the "entry wage") enabled the American automakers to compete globally and led to the industry turn around. In the 2011 auto negotiations, the continuation of some past bargaining concessions was interpreted by the financial community as a sign that the Detroit Three was able to control labor costs and successfully compete on a cost basis with foreign companies (Vlasic 2011).[10] It was reported in 2011 that the state of Michigan, the heart of the domestic auto industry and related manufacturing, was adding jobs for the first time since 2000 (In Michigan, decade of job loss is finally coming to an end 2011).[11]

How else, other than concession bargaining, can public employers deal with swollen employment rolls, huge pension commitments that are coming due, and inflexible work rules? The demands made by employers in ultra-concession may seem to unions to be mean-spirited and overreaching but to employers their demands are first steps in campaigns of moderation. In the private sector, there can be no doubt that in the absence of concession bargaining, employers would have carried out their threats to close plants and offices and lay off workers, and union membership and collective bargaining would have been declined even further than they did. This is why union officers usually "sell" the concession agreement to the union members as a sort of *placeholder* that keeps workers on their jobs and the union as bargaining agent—both big accomplishments in hard times—even if the contract terms are unattractive. In future negotiations there will be better terms. At least by then there will still be workers and their union.

Admittedly some workers and their unions may gain through concession bargaining, but there is a dark side to the new collective ultra-concession bargaining. First, important constitutional rights such as freedom of speech and freedom of assembly can be introduced to the work place by the give-and-take and settlements of collective bargaining. Lewin et al. (2011, 28) summarized the vital role that collective bargaining could play in society: "providing checks and balances in the workplace and society, increasing consumer purchasing power, reducing economic inequity, providing worker voice (including on matters of productivity, public service, and consideration of the disadvantaged in society) and advancing basic constitutional rights…" During the new collective bargaining, however, negotiations between unions and employers cannot reach its full potential because bargaining

---

[10] Bunkley (2011) reports on an auto industry analysis that predicts employment in that industry will return to its prerecession levels by 2015 (an increase of 28 %) and that employment on lower wage tiers of two-tiered wage systems account for 23 % of hourly workers at Chrysler, 17 % at General Motors, and 12 % at Ford.

[11] Uchitelle (2011) described how the creation and expansion of a lower wages tier in a two-tier wage system negotiated with General Electric eventually led to lower labor costs and made the company globally competitive. This resulted in job gains.

becomes a forum for bitter confrontation, cost-cutting, and one-sided demands, rather than a way to jointly resolve competitive problems. For instance, in the 2011 negotiations between Cooper Tire & Rubber and the Steelworkers Union, the employer argued that wage cuts and a two-tier wage system had to be continued for the company to be profitable, while the union wanted concessions to be reversed. What followed was failed mediation, a lock-out, and the use of replacement workers in a dispute that was described by a reporter as an "old-school labor brawl," "a labor battle" and a return to an earlier more combative tone to labor–management relations (Bennett 2011, B1, B2). After 3 months of this bitter fight, the union and employer reached a settlement that had a lump-sum payment and a two-tiered wage system (Bennett 2012).

This brings us to a related and equally dismal point about the new collective bargaining. Lewin et al. (2011) also observed how the concession bargaining of the 1980s could offer only temporary cost relief and could not deal directly with the challenges of international competition and domestic nonunion competition. The new concession bargaining is not built on a common understanding of the need for mutual sacrifice and cooperation, and hence it does not leave a wake of union–management workplace innovation. Rather, it leaves a residue of hostility, of getting even when the time is ripe. It does not nourish the need to find solutions to shared problems. It does not fulfill the potential of collective bargaining as a way for employee voice to flourish in the workplace. Instead, it is mean-spirited and one-sided.

Born of economic hard times and the spread of domestic low-cost competition, I do not expect the new concession bargaining to fade away soon. Ultra-concession bargaining will dominate the labor relations landscape, becoming *how bargaining is done*. Employers will emulate each other and prove their mettle by bargaining tough. There will always be conventional collective bargaining, but it will account for fewer and fewer cases. And it is uncertain whether unions can find alternative ways of representing workers when bargaining has become a losing proposition for them. Will there be a new "bargaining plus," in which unions speak for workers where they work and for working families and the unemployed through local political action (Chaison 2006)? Can a besieged union movement find the will and the way to win back their collective bargaining power and regain all that they have given up, and also find new ways to empower workers? Most likely not. One thing that is clear—after going through two intense waves of concession bargaining, collective bargaining will never be the same.

References

Austen I (2012a) Caterpillar locks out workers in Canada. New York Times http://www.nytimes.com 2 January. Accessed 2 January 2012.

Austen I (2012b) Caterpillar to close assembly factory in Canada. New York Times http://www.nytimes.com 4 February. Accessed 4 February 2012

Baxter S (2011) US agency appeals to California governor to halt rising pension benefits. http://www.fendamentalsmagazine.com 1 March. Accessed 1 March 2011.

Bennett J (2011) Old-School labor brawl erupts at Ohio tire plant. Wall Street Journal 8 December: B1, B2.

Bennett J (2012) Cooper Tire workers back pact. Wall Street Journal. http://www.wsj.com. 29 February. Accessed 29 February 2012.

Bunkley N (2011) Group predicts 28% gain in car making jobs by 2015. New York Times http://www.nytimes.com 30 November. Accessed 30 November 2011.

Carley M et al. (2009) Industrial relations developments in Europe 2009. http://www.eurofound.europa.eu. 28 July. Accessed 6 February 2012.

Chaison G (2006) Unions in America. Sage. Thousand Oaks, California.

Chaison G. (2010) Union membership attrition. Monthly Labor Rev. 133:74-76.

Chaison G and Bigelow B (2002) Unions and legitimacy. Sage, Thousand Oaks CA.

Chaison G and Rose J (1991) The macrodeterminants of union growth and decline. In Strauss et al. (eds.) The state of the unions. Madison, WI. Indust. Rel. Res. Assoc.

Cooper M (2010) Governments go to extremes as the downturn wears on. New York Times http://www.nytimes.com. 6 August. Accessed 6 August 2011.

Detroit, the union and improving times. (2011) New York Times. http://www.nytimes.com 28 July. Accessed 1 August 2011.

Ewing J (2011) VW workers agree to pact bolstering share of profit. New York Times February: B7

Greenhouse S (2011a) A watershed moment for public sector unions. New York Times, 18 February: 14.

Greenhouse S (2011b) Wal-Mart workers try the non-union route. New York Times. http://www.nytimes.com. 14 June. Accessed 15 June 2011.

Greenhouse S (2012) More lockouts as companies battle unions. New York Times. http://www.nytimes.com. 22 January. Accessed 23 January 2012.

Hassel A (2010) Twenty years after German unification: The restructuring of the German welfare and employment regime. German Politics and Soc. 28:102-115.

Hoffman BG (2009) CAW approves deal with Ford. Detroit News http://www.detnews.com. 1 November. Accessed 1 November 2009.

In Michigan, decade of job loss is finally coming to an end. (2011). Detroit Free Press. http://www.freep.com 26 December. Accessed 26 December 2011.

Jones JM (2008) Americans remain broadly supportive of labor unions. http://www.gallup.com.html 1 December. Accessed 2 December 2008.

Kaufman BE (2004) Prospects for union growth in the United States in the early 21st century. In Verma A and Kochan TA (eds) Unions in the 21st century. London, Palgrave-Macmillan.

Landler M (2005) German labor's new reality. New York Times http://www.nytimes.com. 26 October: A1.

Lee D (2011) Two-tier wage system brings reopening of GM plant, reviving hope. Los Angeles Times http://www.latimes.com 18 December. Accessed 18 December 2011.

Lewin D et al (2011) Getting it right: Empirical evidence and policy implications from research on public-sector unionism and collective bargaining. Labor and Employment Research Associations. Employment Policy Research Network http://www.LERA.org. 16 March. Accessed 20 March 2011.

Massa-Wirth H and H Seifert (2005) German pacts for employment and competitiveness: Concessionary bargaining as a reaction to globalisation and European integration. Transfer 11:26-44.

Maher K (2011) Outlook: States' pay cuts present mixed economic blessing. Wall Street Journal 2 May 2011: A2.

Matas R (2010) Pragmatism rules the day at labour talks: Government workers' unions going for job security in exchange for wage freezes. Globe and Mail (Canada) 31 March: S2

Mishel L (1986) The structural determinants of union bargaining power. Ind. Labor Rel. Rev. 40:90–104.

Paddon D (2012) Union pickets Caterpillar dealerships across Canada to protest wage cuts. Canadian Business http://www.canadianbusiness.com 26 January. Accessed 27 January 2012.

Raskin AH (1982) Turnabout in bargaining. Journal of the Institute for Socioeconomic Studies 7: 12-22.

Reich M (2012) *Industrial Relations*: Celebrating and reflecting on fifty-years of publication. Indus. Rel. 51: 1-2

Romig A (2011) Argentine leaders toughens up on union allies. Wall Street Journal 1 December: A16

Rose JB, Chaison GN (1996) Linking union density and union effectiveness: The North-American experience. Indust. Rel. 35: 78-105.

Rose JB, Chaison GN (2001) Unionism in Canada and the United States in the 21st century. Relations industrielles-Indust. Rel. 56: 34-65.

Schmitt J, Mitukiewicz A (2011) Politics matter: Changes in unionization rates in rich countries, 1960-2010. Washington, D.C., Center for Economic Policy and Research.

Traxler F, Brandl B (2009) The economic effects of collective bargaining coverage: A cross-national analysis. Geneva, Switzerland, International Labor Organization.

Tyler T (2009) Employee engagement and union relations. Gallup Management Journal http://www.gmj.gallup.com. 10 September. Accessed 24 May 2012.

Uchitelle L (2011) Factory jobs gain, but wages retreat. New York Times http://www.nytimes.com 29 December. Accessed 30 December 2011.

Union membership and coverage in 2011 (2011). http://www.unionstats.com January. Accessed 24 January 2012.

United States Department of Labor (2012) Union members—2011. Bureau of Labor Statistics. Economic News Release, http://www.bls.gov. 27 January. Accessed 27 January 2012.

Vlasic B (2011) With new labor contracts, Detroit protects turnaround. New York Times http://www.nytimes.com 27 October. Accessed 27 October 2011.

GPSR Compliance

The European Union's (EU) General Product Safety Regulation (GPSR) is a set of rules that requires consumer products to be safe and our obligations to ensure this.

If you have any concerns about our products, you can contact us on ProductSafety@springernature.com

In case Publisher is established outside the EU, the EU authorized representative is:

Springer Nature Customer Service Center GmbH
Europaplatz 3
69115 Heidelberg, Germany

Batch number: 10844675

Printed by Printforce, the Netherlands